NEW ENGLAND'S LIFESAVER

NEW ENGLAND'S LIFESAVER

COAST GUARD LEGEND MASTER CHIEF JACK DOWNEY

Captain W. Russell Webster, USCG (Ret.)
and Captain Michael A. Cicalese, USCGR (Ret.)

THE History PRESS

Published by The History Press
An imprint of Arcadia Publishing
Charleston, SC
www.historypress.com

First published 2025

Manufactured in the United States

ISBN 9781467157414

Library of Congress Control Number: 2025936194

Dedicated to the men and women of the U.S. Coast Guard Boat Forces.

Here and there may be found men in all walks of life who neither wonder or care how much or how little the world thinks of them. They pursue life's pathways, doing their appointed tasks without ostentation, loving their work for work's sake, content to live and do in the present rather than look for uncertain rewards of the future. To them notoriety, distinction, or even fame, acts neither as a spur nor a check to endeavor, yet they are really among the foremost of those who do the world's work.[1]

—Superintendent of the U.S. Life-Saving Service Sumner Increase Kimball, speaking of Joshua James in 1902

CONTENTS

FOREWORD

It was a celebration like no other. When Jack retired in 2008 in a ceremony at Station Point Judith, Rhode Island—close to where he began his venerable Coast Guard career—his impact on the service could be judged by who and how many attended. So many admirals were there that one could not turn around without bumping into one of them, unusual and outside the norm for any enlisted person except for the master chief petty officer of the Coast Guard. The event rivaled a major district or area command retirement and clearly showed the respect and admiration that Coast Guardsmen across the service felt for him.

Then again, we are talking about Jack Downey. Jack had a long, diverse career and extensive leadership experience ashore and afloat in his forty-two years in the Coast Guard, all in New England. His impact was legend and had service-wide impacts that continue even today. His evolution as a leader reached across five decades within three departments—Treasury, Transportation and Homeland Security—under the tenures of eleven commandants.

I have met many exceptional Coast Guard men and women, and I hold them all in great respect. But I can truly say that Jack Downey stands near the top of my personal pantheon of Coast Guard heroes. In truth, almost everyone in the Coast Guard, particularly if they had ever been stationed in the Northeast, has a Jack Downey story. Including me.

After my appointment as the tenth master chief petty officer of the Coast Guard in early 2006, Jack called me at Station Marathon in the Florida Keys.

Vice Admiral Crea and Master Chief Downey at his retirement ceremony. *Defense Information Distribution Service.*

He wanted to know if I thought he should apply to serve as a command master chief.

"Sure, Jack, you would make a great command master chief! But you must do two things," I said.

"What two things?" asked Downey.

"You have to start carrying a cellphone, and you have to answer your own e-mails."

He laughed and said, "Well, I can do that!" So, I told him he should apply.

Soon after, Jack was selected to become the District One, U.S. Northeast region's command master chief. That posting was his last tour of duty, and he did an incredible job!

He had superior communication skills and the ability to "cut to the chase" and get things done. But the one thing that I thought Jack had that was different than almost all other candidates was his demonstrated ability to evolve as a leader.

Jack had a wide range of assignments through his long and storied career, and whether he served in command of multi-mission stations, cutters at sea or as an instructor at the prestigious Command and Operations School at the Coast Guard Academy, he always rose to the occasion and brought something extra to the job. While many of his peers "tapped out" in one type of assignment and became stuck in their ways, unable to change with the times or policies, Jack did not.

This may surprise some readers given Jack's undeniable persona as a rough and gruff boatswain's mate. But he was the Coast Guard's ultimate Renaissance man. He could rise to any occasion and effectively lead, even if it meant answering a cellphone.

When Captains Cicalese and Webster asked me to write the foreword to *New England's Lifesaver* about my friend and mentor Master Chief Jack Downey, I was honored to do so. The original title, *A Sea of Devotion*, was partially selected by Master Chief Downey years ago for the book he never got a chance to write himself. This book eloquently recounts story after story of commitment to his service, which began before we put a man on the moon and continued for several decades and even after he retired. It captures his quiet heroism and enduring influence on future leaders in all ranks. Downey's simple wisdom plays out in detail through the eyes of those whose lives were changed, from his earliest assignment as what is widely believed to be the first time a reservist was asked to transition to active duty (in peacetime), in order to command Station Point Judith in 1979, until well after his 2008 retirement. *New England's Lifesaver* should be required reading for all future leaders throughout the Coast Guard.

—MASTER CHIEF SKIP BOWEN, USCG (Ret.),
Tenth MCPO of the Coast Guard

ACKNOWLEDGEMENTS

To the Downey family for their kindness in sharing Master Chief Downey's personal archives and their remembrances of their loved one.

To Brian Tague, photographer, who provided the lion's share of pictures throughout this book. Brian had documented many modern-era Coast Guard events in the Northeast and remains a critical part of the historic Flying Santa program (https://flyingsanta.org).

Our thanks extend to acquisitions editor Mike Kinsella and his talented team at The History Press for their support and guidance over many months of engagement.

Downey greets Santa Claus as part of the Flying Santa program. *Brian Tague.*

PREAMBLE

In 1784, Dr. Henry Moyes, a blind Scottish chemist, delivered a lecture in Boston about Great Britain's Royal Humane Society, formed in 1774 and renamed the Humane Society in 1776, regarding its work to revive drowning victims.[2]

Within twenty-four hours of hearing Moyes's lecture, Reverend James Freeman obtained a copy of the regulations of the Royal Humane Society. Freeman supplied a copy to Massachusetts Governor James Bowdoin, already familiar with Moyes's lectures. Within hours, Reverend Freeman had transcribed the document for the purpose of raising funds to establish a similar organization.[3]

On January 5, 1786, subscribers to the new regulations met at the Bunch of Grapes Tavern in Boston to discuss an American version of the British model that would create the first procedures to revive drowning victims, including the blowing of warm tobacco smoke up the "fundament" (buttocks). This is where the colloquial phrase "blowing smoke" derives. Governor Bowdoin was the group's first president. Among the original subscribers were Drs. John Warren, Benjamin Waterhouse and Aaron Dexter, who would go on to form the Harvard Medical School in 1782.

As shipping commerce grew in the eighteenth and nineteenth centuries, so, too, did the number of wrecks along the Eastern Seaboard along sparsely populated stretches. Shipwrecked mariners faced the prospect of attempting to swim three to four hundred yards from offshore sandbars in cold Atlantic waters. If they had been fortunate enough to survive the wreck and the chilling swim, they faced death by exposure in most areas. By 1787, the Massachusetts Humane Society had matured and strategically placed three "rescue huts" near approaches to Boston Harbor at Scituate Harbor, Point Allerton and on the west end of Lovell's Island.

The concept was that shipwrecked mariners could take temporary shelter in the huts, burn wood to signal their presence to local citizens and stay warm with blankets and other basic provisions. But pilferage of the huts was an early problem, leading the society to secure "paid guardians" to watch over the buildings, especially during inclement weather when wrecks were more likely to occur. "This arrangement would eventually come to pass, with the professionally staffed lifeboat stations operated by the U.S. Life-Saving Service [USLSS]" decades later.[4]

In 1848, the USLSS was formed by the Newell Act, representing the U.S. government's first formal foray into the lifesaving business by an act of Congress that provided for rockets, lifeboats, carronades (short cannons) and other apparatus on the New Jersey shore. The Humane Society also requested government funding for stations along Massachusetts's coast. The stations were to be administered by the Revenue Marine, a Coast Guard predecessor organization under the Treasury Department. "These stations were run like a volunteer fire department, but without anyone in charge, nor any inspection system to ensure that men and equipment were up to standards."[5]

That would soon change after a disastrous response to an 1854 shipwreck that initiated calls for a greater rescue structure and rigorous oversight. Congress soon appointed funds for a single paid keeper at each station, but that person still had to gather local volunteers at the sailor's moment of greatest need. The Civil War stalled efforts to upgrade the lifesaving service until Sumner I. Kimball, the newly appointed director of the Revenue Marine Division in the Treasury Department in 1871, ordered an inspection of the lifesaving network. The report was damning and led to Congress authorizing $200,000 for the first paid surfmen and to build stations where needed.[6]

What followed was a complete overhaul of the rescue system under the watchful eye of Kimball and the Revenue Cutter Service (RCS), the renamed Revenue Marine Division, in the Treasury Department. Stations were named, numbered and regularly inspected by district superintendents. Now, members of the USLSS were paid, and in 1891, they wore formal uniforms that distinguished their rank and purpose. Lifeboats and modern equipment were provided at each station. Routines were created that ensured conformance to standards. Daily station activities provided consistency throughout the service.

Mondays and Thursdays were devoted to drilling with equipment needed for rescues attempted from the beach, such as the Lyle gun and breeches buoy. Tuesdays featured lifeboat and surfboat drills, with at least a half an hour using the oars. Wednesday was signaling day, when crews practiced with flags and flares for communications with stranded ships. Friday's training was designated for giving first aid to drowned mariners. Saturdays were devoted to the grounds and station upkeep, and Sundays were days of rest.[7]

Point Allerton's Keeper Joshua James bridged two organizations, the Massachusetts Humane Society and the U.S. Life-Saving Service. He is acknowledged as his era's most significant rescuer, with more than six hundred lives saved. He and his crew were awarded the Gold Lifesaving Medal on January 10, 1889, for saving thirteen lives on the schooners *Gertrude Abbott* and *H.C. Higginson* over a two-day rescue on November 25–26, 1888. James's career as a rescuer began at age fifteen and continued for sixty years. By 1886, the Humane Society had struck a special silver medal to commemorate his "faithful service of more than 40 years."[8]

Among the USLSS's notable involvements in history, Kill Devil Hills surfman J.T. Daniels took the photograph that documented the Wright brothers' flight using a heavier-than-air machine on December 17, 1903. The crew at the station assisted the Wrights in all three subsequent flights that day by carrying the plane back to the starting point. The U.S. Life-Saving Service created 280 lifesaving stations along the Atlantic and Pacific coasts and the Great Lakes. By 1915, when the service was assimilated into the newly formed Coast Guard, "the rescuers of the United States Life-Saving Service—fishermen, lobstermen, crabbers, and others who grew up along America's shores—had saved more than 186,000 lives, becoming collectively the greatest institution of their kind in the world."

Downey wearing his ceremonial cap upon being honored as the Coast Guard's first Ancient Keeper, November 2003. *Brian Tague.*

On January 20, 1915, President Woodrow Wilson signed into law an act that combined the USLSS and the Revenue Cutter Service,

Commandant Tom Collins pins Master Chief Downey's Ancient Keeper badge on his uniform. *Brian Tague.*

thereby creating the U.S. Coast Guard.[9] The modern-day Coast Guard acknowledged Joshua James as its historical icon and preserved his memory and his legacy with a prestigious award, presented to

> *a Coast Guard member on Active Duty in recognition of their longevity and outstanding performance in Coast Guard boat operations. The Joshua James Ancient Keeper Award's namesake, Keeper Joshua James, is the most celebrated lifesaver in Coast Guard history with 626 lives saved. The "Ancient Keeper" award represents all keepers who continue to live by the creed of those that have served before them. They continue to go to the sea's rocky realm at extreme peril to their own lives, in pursuit of the safety and security of others, in performance of our Coast Guard missions. Today, the Ancient Keeper is charged with keeping the oversight of Coast Guard boat operations to ensure the services tradition of professionalism remains intact.*[10]

Master Chief Jack Downey's legacy and prowess as a leader in the Boat Forces led him to be named the first Ancient Keeper Award recipient. These are his stories.

PROLOGUE

Coast Guard senior and master chiefs—the highest-tier noncommissioned personnel—lead the enlisted ranks, providing wisdom, experience and practical know-how and enabling officers to undertake the service's missions with core values of honor, respect and devotion to duty. Chiefs are the consummate connective tissue between officer and enlisted. Our friend Master Chief John E. "Jack" Downey, who passed on August 17, 2022, was one such leader, unforgettable and unique. His death following a long illness left a void among a hefty network of friends, colleagues and a large, loving family.

We wrote *New England's Lifesaver* to recount stories of friendship and family and to fortify Jack's legacy of leadership, including accounts of Downey's hard-driving ways, humor, his skilled mentorship and his days as a tough taskmaster who trumpeted truth without the benefit of filters. Chapter 2's title, "A Sea of Devotion," must be credited to Downey, as it came from his partially completed autobiography with that name. The preamble provides the evolution of lifesaving endeavors in New England to set the stage for comparing how past pioneers of these noble endeavors compare with Master Chief Downey's legacy of deeds and actions.

In most instances, Downey's leadership methods, although sometimes viewed as draconian, are remarkably like heroes and legends of the past, including the Coast Guard's most famous rescuer, Keeper Joshua James. What separates the legends is Downey's evolutionary adaptability to change and his ability to revolutionize his entire service's rescue procedures throughout a portion of five decades in service. He also paid significant homage to the historic icons he worshiped and the artifacts of our service's history and emulated past heroes right up until the time of his passing.

Filled with compelling firsthand accounts written by men and women who worked with Downey, this book is our way of saying "fair winds and following seas" to a dear friend and to leave a truthful imprint of Jack's leadership style—from unvarnished to virtue—for those who will never meet him. To do this, we gathered and curated memories and yarns of Jack via a link on Captain Webster's author website and combed through Jack's extensive personal archives at his home near Point Judith, Rhode Island; newspaper articles; and official Coast Guard records. For many who submitted recollections of Jack, letter after letter acknowledged that their lives were changed for the better under his leadership, even after an initial bitter disappointment when a service member failed a certification thanks to Jack's unusually high standards. While acknowledging the disappointment, most admitted that they were better off having known Downey.

A CHIEF FOR THE AGES

Downey, the Coast Guard's first Ancient Keeper, retired in 2008 following a storied forty-two-year career in Coast Guard District One (Northeast) beginning in 1966. Throughout, Downey, who is credited with saving more than seven hundred lives, witnessed transformational change in his beloved service. He served under eleven commandants and was officer in charge at thirteen boat forces (rescue) stations and cutters, serving twenty-eight years at Northeast operational commands. He witnessed and adapted to shifts in Coast Guard culture, its character and advances in technology ranging from radio technology to newer classes of rescue ships. During Downey's time, the Coast Guard was overseen by the Treasury Department, later the Transportation Department and, finally, after 9/11, the Department of Homeland Security, where the service resides today. He experienced and thrived through no fewer than three uniform changes and an equal number of cultural shifts, each with their own challenges and adaptations. He transitioned through them all and led four generations of guardsmen.

Some two years after Jack died, retired Senior Chief Gordie McClay, with whom Downey had worked closely for years and who became a trusted friend, remembered, "Sometimes, Downey's leadership style was unorthodox, but always with good reason and positive outcomes. I learned a lot more than

Left to right: Senior Chief Lucey, Warrant Officer Guthlein, Master Chief Downey and Senior Chief McClay pose at the Hull Lifesaving Museum, November 2003. *Brian Tague.*

search and rescue and boat handling. I learned that people are the greatest asset and if everyone works as a team anything is possible. He had a work ethic like no other, he was dedicated to the Coast Guard and his family. He knew when anyone was trying to cut corners or pull the wool over his eyes. That was a mistake you only made once. He magically knew what you were doing at the station, even if he was at home. When your tour was over, you were a different person compared to when you checked in."

Downey was old school, leavened with resilience in evolving times. His leadership style merged age-old seafaring ways with contemporary expectations of an evolving service dedicated to saving human lives at risk on the sea. Jack mentored hundreds. He fought to upgrade Boat Forces' personal protection equipment and create and adopt new small station Green-Amber-Red risk assessment models, and he had a deep respect for his service's heritage.

Known as "Chief Fix-It," Downey managed two or three units as the acting officer in charge, sometimes simultaneously. A quick scan of Appendix 9 will reveal how many temporary and permanent commands the master chief held, both ashore and afloat. In fact, holding dual commands would become a hallmark in his career. Downey personally tested newly designed shallow-water, jet-drive, surf-capable small boats, maneuvering these vessels every which way over, sideways and into waves. After he'd become a master chief, when some might have stayed comfortable on past credibility, he challenged himself to become surf qualified so that he would know how to lead his charges over the Chatham Bar. In short, Master Chief Downey innovated solutions in unorthodox ways and not through established Coast Guard standards or procedures. While his career was formally acknowledged by many awards, including the Navy League of the United States' Munro Award and the Coast Guard's first Joshua James Ancient Keeper's Award in honor of a service historical rescue icon, his greatest reward was seeing those he had trained excel beyond even their own expectations. Retired CWO Thomas Guthlein, another protégé and long-standing friend, was the first National Motor Life Boat School instructor from the East Coast, and retired Senior Chief Sheila Lucey, a third protégé and long-standing friend, was the first woman to be surfman qualified. Downey's legacy was one of consistent leadership and adapting to change.

Leadership was always on Downey's mind. He began by having a coffee, discussing a particular case or something that was bothering him. But in

Downey's family members at his Ancient Keeper ceremony. *From left to right*: Judith, Jack, Commandant Collins, Jennifer, Jayson, Justyn, Ryan and Rebecca. *Brian Tague.*

time, the discussions slowly drifted to the topic of leadership. The *New York Times* bestseller *Leadership Lessons of Attila the Hun*, by Wess Roberts, was part of his personal library.

Captain Cicalese met MCPO Downey on *Chase* when he was a lieutenant junior grade. From that initial tour, they maintained a friendship for more than forty years, trading stories, drinking coffee or working through a problem that was gnawing at one of them. Cicalese, who was a licensed SCUBA instructor in five disciplines, including rescue, and held mixed-gas salvage diving officer credentials, recalled a conversation that at the time he considered peculiar because it focused on only wet suits and dry suits, not driving boats or the Coast Guard. Jack never stopped considering new or better solutions, seeking to pass his learning along.

Captain Webster met Master Chief Downey in July 1998, shortly after taking command of Group Woods Hole, one of the largest and most active search and rescue areas in the nation, spanning from the Connecticut–Rhode Island border to Duxbury, Massachusetts, and out two hundred nautical miles. Typically, there were some 1,250 SAR cases each year, many occurring in the summer months when tourists and locals alike put their boats in for an afternoon of fun. It was a time when "summer fun" still, tragically, meant cigarette boats hopping from one local harbor to the next and playing a drinking game involving poker, with the loser buying everyone a round before proceeding to the next port of call. It was a different time. I'll never forget the police chief of one small Rhode Island town acknowledging that his threshold for law enforcement's involvement in a boating DUI was "if someone dies."

There were challenges at the Group, including the ongoing discussions about the right mix of boats capable of operating in the surf at Station Chatham and maintaining the proper qualifications for the guardsmen who operated on the shifting sands of the Chatham Bar. I knew I had to meet the master chief and get his perspective on the issues—issues so significant and part of the community fabric that the Chatham Town Council had seen fit to assign Parker Wiseman as its official Coast Guard liaison. Wiseman proved a tough advocate for both the town and the Coast Guard, walking a political tightrope. My first conversation with the master chief covered a wide range of topics, including how to safely operate in such a treacherous environment. The master chief took me to their nearby station Chatham boathouse, where a forty-four-foot motor lifeboat (MLB) was being worked on.

He pointed out the propeller blades of the MLB sitting in the cradle and articulated the hazards of operating near the ever-shifting sand channels leading out from the Chatham Bar area. The blades were all shiny, obviously sand blasted by having been run through the sand for many trips to and from the nearby Atlantic waters. Knowing that every time a boat had run aground, stations were required to submit a formal "grounding" report, I asked to review those reports for any insights, having recently been a deputy group commander up until three years prior in southern Maine. Running aground in Maine resulted in a very different and serious review by senior leadership.

But the master chief took my question in stride and simply said, "Captain, if we filed a grounding report every time the MLB ran aground on the Chatham Bar, we'd do little else except prepare grounding reports!"

These stories describe a man always on the highest standard for himself, and he expected the same for those who worked with him or for him; he continuously examined the status quo with the belief that it might be made better. A harbor master who worked with Downey during a troubled time said it best: "Jack saved everyone and everything."

Others disagreed. In truth, some who responded to our request for "Downey stories" were reluctant to do so on the record. Several privately expressed anger at the master chief's leadership style, which they said was rigid at times or unfair. Not everyone agreed with his management style. A few others said that it was tough for women to work with Jack. And some claimed that Downey could be hardheaded and heavy-handed and considered his quest for perfection too inflexible. Others still actively attempted to dissuade us from writing this book.

Jack would be the first to admit that he wasn't perfect. Working for him wasn't all happy times and positive reflections. Our research revealed a small minority of respondents who wished to remain anonymous who faulted Jack for his occasional "old-school" and sometimes harsh methodologies. Most recollections were from decades ago—a different time and place—while remembering and evaluating his actions through today's different cultural lenses using modern metrics. But we knew all his sides, and we knew that he was truly one of the last old-school master chiefs. Many of the actions he undertook wouldn't pass in our culture. And the way he occasionally behaved would not be accepted in today's world. But we also have written about past service icons who exhibited human characteristics that would be frowned on and be cause for criticism or outright cancelation. And yet past leaders have seen fit to name buildings and cutters after these flawed heroes.

Coast Guard cutter *Eagle* at the U.S. Coast Guard Academy, New London, Connecticut, where Downey instructed at the Leadership and Development Center, circa 2000. *USCG photo.*

During Jack's time, Coast Guard protocols shifted toward tightening standards of conduct and dress. Beards were banned, and drinking in uniform and in public became frowned upon, as were some tattoos. A focus to stop smoking and weight restrictions accompanied new health standards that were enforced. Random drug testing, new uniforms and updated equipment all became part of a savvier Guard "working smarter not harder." Some of this he occasionally questioned, especially when his tour at one station was shortened to solve a problem at another unit. "Change can be confusing and takes time," he once said, "something commands can't manufacture." In a bit of irony, services were embracing those with beards and tattoos, in addition to other signs of a relaxed military framework at the time this book was written.

Jack remembered when he was interviewed for a job to train cadets at the Coast Guard Academy. He did not want the position. But the Academy wanted Downey. The powers that be felt that cadets should have a greater appreciation for the enlisted men and women they would one day lead. The onboarding process did not begin well. Jack told the hiring official, "I don't text. I don't read my e-mails, and I have trouble with computers."

Downey and First District Commander Rear Admiral Tim Sullivan discuss a picture of service icon Joshua James. *Brian Tague.*

But they brought him aboard anyway. Jack spent four years in New London, Connecticut. His lectures—complemented by Jack's animated and captivating storytelling style—were some of the most popular given at the Academy and are still recalled fondly by today's staff. He'd color up the sea tales and mix in anecdotes that entertained the cadets and faculty yet taught them invaluable lessons. Jack led "up" into the officer corps, the same way he led those men and women in his own commands.

Jack's blunt and honest demeanor, while off-putting to some, steadied the careers of many. These qualities were emblematic of the way he interacted with juniors and superiors alike. For more than four decades, Master Chief Downey set out to save lives and bring his crews home safe and sound. He didn't just train crews needed to work Coast Guard missions. He influenced many a crew member so that years later, when retired and out of uniform, they would recount their days in uniform and their life after Downey, giving thanks to him for having such a positive impact on them.

Downey remains in living memory as an imperfect man but perfectly legendary. During Master Chief Downey's 2008 retirement ceremony, First District Commander Rear Admiral Tim Sullivan struggled with the notion of calling anyone a legend and began with the definition: "Legend, a story or body of stories, handed down for generations and popularly believed to have a historical basis."[11] The admiral went on to quantify to the more than five hundred guests how the master chief, now recently retired, had already achieved the status.

We each maintained a personal friendship with Master Chief Downey throughout our careers and into retirement. No matter where Downey was assigned, we kept in touch through visits or phone calls over the years. Downey was straight out of Central Casting. You couldn't come up with a character who was more seasoned, wise-cracking, smart and excellent at what he did, but he was also someone who could fit into an old film like Frank Capra's *Captains Courageous*. In that 1937 film, Spencer Tracey played the crusty but kind and plain-spoken mariner named Manuel Fidello. Jack was our Manuel. These are Jack Downey's stories.

INTRODUCTION

Master Chief Downey's early years, including a boyhood lived largely outdoors, are covered in this book's opening chapters. The second chapter, "A Sea of Devotion," is a tribute to Downey's own unfinished autobiography with the same name. Like it did in so many other aspects of his life, "self" came second to service and his beloved and cherished family.

The middle segments document the bulk of Jack's storied career, including achievements, awards and personal aspects of his time with the Coast Guard. The final sections recount his retirement years, including contributions to service heritage and his persistence to carry on despite declining physical health, as well as, following Downey's death, the movement to name a Coast Guard Boat Forces' Unit Award, a building and possibly a cutter in his honor. There's also a hefty bonus of appendices by family and shipmates.

Downey was New England born and bred, raised on the edge of Rhode Island's south shore, hearing stories from his father's friends who fished for a living. He became even more curious about life at sea after learning how colonists were dependent on ships moving spices and goods from Asia, England and other parts of America. The whaling industry based in nearby New Bedford and on Nantucket also fascinated a young Jack. By high school, he understood how important and dangerous shipping and the sea were. A history class revealed how Alexander Hamilton founded the U.S. Revenue Marine (later the Revenue Cutter Service) in 1790 to prevent smuggling, to enforce trade and tariff laws and to protect American waterways. The U.S. Coast Guard was created in 1915 following the mergers between the Revenue Cutter Service and U.S. Life-Saving Service.

Downey became more curious about the local Coast Guard station, Station Point Judith, which existed a "life ring's throw away" in the shadows of the Downey household. He immersed himself in learning about the organization and was captivated by Joshua James, who by 1841 was already a renowned lifesaver. Little did he know then that the U.S. Coast Guard would become an enormous part of his life, second only to his family. Joshua sailed at an early age with his father and older brothers, all of whom worked for the family's shipping business, transporting paving stones to Boston on schooners they owned. Downey studied James's career from the Humane Society of the Commonwealth of Massachusetts to the U.S. Life-Saving Service and his miraculous rescue after rescue; by the time James died during a training session in 1902 at the age of seventy-five, he had amassed 626 rescues.

Downey is believed to have been the first reservist called to active duty in peacetime in June 1979. This action opened the door for reservists to augment active-duty personnel beyond their customary wartime mobilization orders.

Jack's respect and advocacy for service heritage caused him to rub shoulders with many whom he respected and admired. Retired Chief Warrant Officer Bernie Webber was at the top of Downey's list. Webber retired in 1966, the year Jack enlisted. But it wouldn't be until the 1980s that their paths crossed

Station Point Judith. *Brian Tague.*

whenever Webber visited Station Chatham on Cape Cod, where Jack was officer in charge (OIC). An icon himself, Webber was coxswain of the venerable CG36500, a thirty-six-foot vintage surfboat that was used to rescue thirty-two merchant mariners from the foundering oil tanker *Pendleton* off Chatham on February 18, 1952. The type T2 tanker, which merchant mariners derisively nick named "Kaiser coffins" for their propensity to split in half, had split in two during a nor'easter. A second T2, the *Fort Mercer*, had also broken in half that same evening and had diverted Coast Guard deepwater rescue cutters, complicated the rescue and limited *Pendleton*'s crew's chances to one small boat with a ramshackle crew led by Webber.

Downey and Webber bonded over stories of that '52 rescue, which made global headlines. Members of the Orleans Historical Society, the eventual owners (now known as the Centers for Cultural and History in Orleans), found the orphaned and decaying CG36500 in a landfill and rescued it. Over time, Downey and available Coast Guard crewmen, along with members of the Orleans Historical Society, refurbished the vessel. Downey even went so far as to bring the venerable boat with him from Chatham to his next assignment on Nantucket so that he could keep the tradition alive and maintain the vessel. Webber was the last person whom Downey acknowledged during formal ceremonies honoring the seventieth anniversary of the famous rescue in 2022, six months before the master chief's death.

Like Webber, who regarded Joshua James in high esteem, Downey regarded both James and Webber the same way. Several of Downey's protégés—namely Warrant Officer Tom Guthlein, Senior Chief Sheila Lucey and Senior Chief Gordie McClay—saw Jack as more than just another man sharing the same uniform. Some of their stories with and about the master chief are told in this book and validate his influence.

Jack's interactions with his senior command leaders "didn't always go the way the senior person thought it would go but ultimately Master Chief Downey was helping that senior person learn, know what the real story was, and help them to be a better leader. He was an honest man to a fault which sometimes led to trust issues but ultimately if he knew you were in it for the right reasons, he would bring you into the fold."[12]

Downey's influence was so fanatical that members who had not worked directly with or for Downey but who had heard of him only from friends and colleagues spoke of him more as a legend than a living Coast Guard colleague. It is our hope that readers get to know Master Chief Downey as we have had the pleasure and honor of knowing him.

Downey holding a spoof picture of him with his three protégés—Lucey, McClay and Guthlein—all wearing an Ancient Keeper cap. *Brian Tague.*

Downey's considerable influence included the two authors of this book. Parts of this book are extracted from their own direct interactions with the master chief over a combined sixty-four years. Captain Cicalese, who knew Downey for the better part of four decades, was the master chief's supervisor on the bridge and for boardings when he was chief of the boat in cutter *Chase*. He also knew the master chief from his time in the reserves and was part of the District One team that created the district's first operational risk management instructions in 2003. Captain Cicalese also saw the master chief frequently when he visited Boston's Mariners House, where Cicalese was the executive director for nearly twenty years.

Captain Webster was the group commander of Woods Hole from 1998 to 2001, when Downey simultaneously commanded several of his units. Webster was also the MISHAP Analysis Board president for the 2001 Station Niagara tragedy, where two guardsmen perished, and Downey played a pivotal role in establishing the timeline for the accident, leading to twenty-two national boat forces' recommendations, including full funding for immersion suits for all Coast Guard cold weather stations. The master chief and Captain Webster also were part of a small volunteer team that organized the fiftieth anniversary celebrations of the 1952 *Pendleton* rescue crew and their families. Webster, along with his wife and Downey, also toured New England maritime institutions from 2007 to 2015, retelling the *Pendleton* rescue story to more than seven thousand cadets and others.

Throughout the book's narrative, you will see that the authors took some liberties in their characterization of the master chief, alternatively calling him "Master Chief Downey," "Downey," "the master chief" and occasionally just "Jack." Up until the time of his death, and true to form, Master Chief Downey called both authors "Captain" and nothing else.

Chapter 1

BOOKENDS OF A LEGEND'S LIFE

Slowly, on a warm late summer morning on Monday, August 29, 2022, a line of vehicles meandered toward Saint Mary's Star of the Sea Catholic Church in Narragansett, Rhode Island. The parking lot was packed as the family of John E. "Jack" Downey began the process of honoring the retired master chief. Downey's distinguished forty-two-year career included saving more than seven hundred people and being the inaugural title holder of the Coast Guard's first Ancient Keeper.

The procession passed Downey's second home—Station Point Judith—on the way to the Rhode Island Veterans' Memorial Cemetery in Exeter. And then something remarkable happened. Approaching and around the Rose Nulman Park turnabout, Coast Guard crews numbering close to two hundred stood at attention and saluted the passing hearse. Along with the Coast Guard crews, there were bystanders, many fishermen among them, who also assembled in line. Some held their hat over their heart, while others saluted. Later, at the grave site, a priest led prayers, and several family members addressed mourners. Each of Jack's five adult children read several lines of a poem, "En Voyage," by Carlyle Emery, honoring their father. "En Voyage" had been given to Downey by his mother a decade earlier following the passing of his father.

Jack's death created a void in both his families—the Downey clan and the Coast Guard. But who was this dynamic, charismatic, brave and tough master chief whom many both feared and loved? John E. "Jack" Downey was born on July 16, 1947, to James and Patricia Doyle Downey. Jack's father was "Big Jim" Downey to those who knew the U.S. Navy and World War II veteran. After the war, Big Jim worked as a plumber and relocated his young family from East Providence to Point Judith, to a cozy bungalow with hot running water and a toilet—real luxuries of the time.[13]

Master Chief John Downey. Photo used in his memorial service, August 2022. *Defense Information Distribution Service, original photo by Lauren Downs, USCG.*

Downey grew up living next to Coast Guard Station Point Judith. His family's home was in Narragansett, "right next to the station—where he saved his first life—a fisherman in distress, and was the officer in charge in 1979 and again in 1998."[14] When Downey was six, his father took him and his older brother Jim to a nearby beach, which featured twenty-foot-high waves during a hurricane, where strong winds lifted the buoys like a circus ride. Downey and the sea became lifelong companions. In formative years, one could find him watching local Coast Guardsmen practicing search and rescue drills or at local docks where fishing crews unloaded their catches. By the time young Downey was ten, he could identify every fishing vessel out of Point Judith or Galilee.[15]

A decent student, Jack was challenged more by interest or disinterest of a subject rather than an ability to learn. Fractions weren't important compared to how many pounds of tautog the *Lady D* crew caught or what a full fish box, iced down, weighed. Jack had an easygoing manner and quick wit that made him a popular classmate. Neither the class clown nor introvert, Downey wasn't shy about sharing his funny bone. His older brother Jim and younger brother Michael both laughed when they recalled a story of why he was so popular: "In those days, 'muscle cars' were all the rage. Many of the guys drove their made-over autos to school. They paraded them around the high school parking lot, revving the engines, wooing all the girls, while irritating the teachers. Jack didn't have that kind of money, neither did our parents. So, in his funny way, he borrowed a friend's horse, rode it to school, tied it up to the school's flagpole, not far from all the parked 'muscle' cars."[16]

Downey's love for boats and the sea bordered on the hypnotic and was in his bones. In high school, Downey had it in his mind to join the local fishing fleet, encouraged as he was by working at the Fisherman's Co-Op located "a life-ring throw away" from Station Point Judith. Downey's father tried to "talk sense into him and convince him otherwise," stating that commercial fishing was a hard life, coupled with the risk that sometimes there might not be a paycheck.[17] Being a plumber was safer and the money more consistent.

Downey met Judith Boardman at his cousin's summer house during a teen get-together, which included drinks and snacks, telling stories and dancing on the deck. Teen sweethearts Jack and Judith, who was raised in Providence, attended different high schools, although Judith knew Downey's cousin Cathy.

After graduating from high school, nineteen-year-old Jack enlisted in the Coast Guard in November 1966. Just out of boot camp at Cape May, New Jersey, in March 1967, Seaman Apprentice Downey reported to his first assignment aboard the Coast Guard cutter *Casco*. Commissioned in 1941, she was a 311-foot Barnegat-class small seaplane tender inherited from the U.S. Navy in 1949. Although aged, she was seaworthy, had comfortable living accommodations and was rigged for long voyages. More importantly, she was homeported in Boston not far from family. (Jack and Judith were married in 1967 and would share fifty-four years of marriage before Downey passed in 2022.)

Less than a year later, in December 1967, a newlywed Downey transferred to Air Station Salem, where he drove a rescue boat to support the Coast Guard's Albatross sea rescue planes. This meant that Downey had to clear and maintain an open sea lane of recreational vessels and be underway in the general vicinity during the planes' takeoffs and landings.

One year later, in the spring of 1968, Downey was again transferred, this time to Station Point Judith in Rhode Island, his family's backyard. There, Downey rotated between reserve and active-duty assignments between 1968 and 1982. These were indeed the rough-and-ready years, when the young couple was just starting out.

A Step Back from Full-Time Coast Guard Duties

While Downey embraced his Coast Guard duties, family took precedence. Judith was pregnant by the time he transferred back to the reserves in November 1970, less than three years after first enlisting. One month later, their daughter Jennifer was born. Jack and Judith were ecstatic; they were back home, and Downey—on the advice of both his father and father-in-law—went back to civilian life and plumbing with his father. Both had convinced Downey to follow in his father's footsteps, saying, "Someone in the trades would never starve." Downey's father mentioned that he could use the help, while Jack's father-in-law politely reminded Jack that now that he was married, he had other responsibilities.[18]

Jack and Judy's second child, Heather, was born in 1973. Shawn, their third, arrived in 1974. Jack and Judith had their family. Jack's parents, James and Patricia, lived nearby, as did all of Jack's siblings. Downey's father, Big Jim, had his favorite helper, his son Jack, now also a licensed master plumber. To satisfy his desire to be at sea, Downey continued his reserve duty at Station Point Judith.

All along, from 1966, when he first enlisted, to when he retired, Downey had two families—the Coast Guard and his own clan. But make no mistake, Judith and their children—Jennifer, Heather, Shawn and twins Ryan and Rebecca—always came first, followed by his siblings James, Tricia, Patience and Michael.

During the five years that Downey split his work time plumbing and serving in the reserves, he juggled the demands of raising a family, running the family's plumbing business and serving in the Coast Guard Reserves. Judith saw to the family's needs. She admitted, "These were difficult times, but Jack always believed in 'Quality Time vs. Quantity Time.' There were fishing excursions, walks on the beach, drives around town for ice cream, and baseball games, intertwined with life's lessons as the kids, and later, his grandchildren, grew."[19]

Years on, Captain Mark Campbell, USCG (Ret.), a fellow cutter man (a Coast Guard designation for those with more than five years of sea duty), spoke of his time with Downey: "In addition to his many professional accomplishments in the Coast Guard, Jack Downey was also a devoted husband and proud parent who greatly appreciated the people surrounding him and wasn't reluctant to express his feelings on that matter." During his change of command of CGC *Hammerhead* (circa 2006), he began his departing remarks with "Instead of 'last but not least,' I want to begin with 'First and Foremost'—my family, because without their love, understanding and support I would not have been able to do this job."[20] In words gifted to an upcoming leader who would succeed him in service, Downey said it best, remembering those who had come before him and his own mortality: "Always look aft before moving ahead, look for people in your wake—make sure they are productive, safely surfing the waves of your wake and not just trying to survive turbulence.…Make sure they recognize your wake as a safe and productive course to follow not just a sign of your departure. Remember that the present becomes the past and that the present and past are a gift to the future. Always remember that your performance and how you work for and with people, coupled with your good deeds in the present, will become the past and your gift and legacy to the future."[21]

Chapter 2

A SEA OF DEVOTION

Living close to Station Point Judith made Downey's Coast Guard Reserve career easier to navigate, especially with a young family and his schedule as a plumber. The commute took just minutes, not hours, allowing an occasional quick trip home to help Judith with the kids in an emergency. And the station knew it could count on Downey to augment a crew or stand a radio watch all on short notice.

With time and persistence, Downey advanced to chief petty officer in September 1975 as a reservist, a unique achievement of his time. Downey's professionalism and leadership were noted by the commandant and documented in a letter of commendation, dated July 16, 1976:

> *I note with pride and am pleased to commend you for your performance of duty during the period April 1975 to December 1975, while serving as Executive Petty Officer, Reserve Unit Pt. Judith, R.I. When the officer in charge, USCG Station, Point Judith, Rhode Island, initiated an accelerated training program for reservists to better qualify them for augmentation you were instrumental in getting the program started.*
>
> *You volunteered your free time to develop and prepare much of the training syllabus necessary to execute this training. More important than that, however, was your dynamic leadership, which was the driving force that made the program a success. In addition to this you provided much needed support for the regular forces at Pt. Judith by scheduling your personal services as the station OOD, SAR Boat Coxswain or SAR Crewman as the need arose.*[22]

Three years later, in 1978, Downey was promoted to senior chief boatswain's mate, again as a reservist. By this time, the Downeys had been married eleven years. Then something changed, shifting Downey's personal and career trajectories.

Between house calls for his plumbing business or when stopping for coffee, Downey often heard locals bash Coast Guard Station Point Judith. Rumor had it that the station was poorly led, which angered Downey.

He knew that the station was not running at peak, but it was a surprise when the commanding officer of Group Woods Hole asked him to return to active duty to take command of Station Point Judith in December 1979. By then, plumbing had lost its luster, and active duty gave Downey an opportunity to lead and drive boats while not owning one, something he could not afford with a growing family. He could not resist.

But there was a hitch. He had to agree to take a demotion from senior chief (E-8) to chief petty officer (E7), a huge gamble and sacrifice. Downey countered with his own stipulation. Downey insisted that the group commander support him *regardless of the problem or solution*, a risky maneuver for both Downey and the group commander. The group commander proposed to bring a reservist to active duty to solve problems the active-duty command could not, but the group commander also plucked that reservist from the ranks and placed him in charge of the personnel he had broken bread with for the last twelve years.

The gamble paid off, and Downey began a full-time tenure as officer in charge of Station Point Judith on December 5, 1979. Overlooking Block Island Sound, Station Point Judith supported a thriving seasonal pleasure-craft community transiting to Block Island to the southeast and Newport to the northeast. Downey insisted that the station support the year-round fishing fleet from the nearby ports of Galilee and Jerusalem—fishermen who a decade before had been closely linked to the Coast Guard. In 1980, Downey initiated dockside safety boardings, wisely claiming, "Why wait until you're at sea and in trouble to find out that you don't have the right gear or know how to use it."[23]

Downey spent the next two years righting Station Point Judith, while integrating himself into active-duty status. In doing so, he became the first Coast Guard reservist called to active duty in peacetime, forever changing how reserve forces could be used beyond wartime service. Downey received his first commendation medal, which read, in part, "Point Judith Station was responsible for the successful completion of over 600 Search and Rescue cases….His exceptional competence in handling personnel problems as well

Coast Guard cutter *Chase*. *USCG photo.*

as Search and Rescue in an effective manner is shown by the high morale of the crew and the 'outstanding' evaluations received in District inspections. In addition, Chief Downey has been instrumental in fostering outstanding public relations within the local community and has enhanced the reputation of Coast Guard Station Point Judith and the Coast Guard."[24]

After two years at Station Point Judith, Downey was transferred in 1982 to the cutter *Chase*, a high-endurance cutter homeported in Boston. Downey saw this as an opportunity to broaden his skill set and advance his career. It had been fifteen years since Downey had served on his first ship, the *Casco*, right out of boot camp. Until 1982, Downey's career had focused on small boat operations. But he understood that to remain competitive with his new active-duty peers, he needed to broaden his experiences.

Judith explained to her husband that she and the children would remain at the family's home base in Rhode Island. The years aboard *Chase*, however, proved challenging for both Judith and Jack. She was alone in caring for five children, ages eleven, eight and seven, with two two-year-olds, all along answering the inevitable question: "When is Daddy coming home?"

Chapter 3

CHIEF OF THE BOAT (COB)

Chief Downey reported as chief of the boat (COB) to the Boston-based cutter *Chase* in 1982. The ship was 378 feet long with sleek lines, a 42-foot beam and two diesel and two gas turbine engines or combined diesel and gas turbines; she had a top speed of thirty-five knots on both JT-4 jet turbines. COBs on Coast Guard cutters performed all the normal duties of a chief petty officer that led a division like "Deckies," or boatswains, those who work on deck, but he was also recognized as the most experienced advisor to the command staff on issues involving the entire cutter, including its operations and people.

Named for Salmon P. Chase, secretary of the treasury between 1861 and 1864 during the Lincoln administration, the ship was launched in 1967 from Avondale Shipyard in Louisiana and came down the ways as the fourth of twelve new Hamilton-class high-endurance cutters.

Designed for speed, comfort and distance, the Hamilton-class cutters were ideal for long-range mid-ocean search and rescue operations, offshore maritime law enforcement fishery and drug-interdiction patrols and anti-submarine warfare and convoy escort operations. The latter two missions were strategically important during the Cold War between the Soviet Union and United States and its NATO allies. With variable-pitch propellers, automatic radio direction finders, extensive secure communications capabilities, an active sonar and advanced air and surface radars, *Chase*'s speed and maneuverability were envied by most other ships manned by Coast Guard personnel. The Coast Guard even briefly experimented with the notion of installing a Harpoon anti-ship missile on one prototype cutter. The ships, now all transferred to other nations and retired from U.S. Coast Guard service, had a complement of 140 enlisted, 12 officers and 12 chief petty officers, managing the versatile *Chase*'s operations worldwide.

The ship's credo was "No Challenge Too Great." The commanding officer of *Chase*, Captain Douglas Currier, was a man who spent more time at sea than at home and was fond of saying, "Underway was the only way." The transfer as chief of the boat aboard *Chase* was critical to Downey's career under two commanding officers, Captains Currier and Lockwood. But Downey was clearly out of his comfort level. He had gone from serving at Station Point Judith for fourteen years, eventually matriculating to its officer in charge, to the single most important enlisted man for many in *Chase*'s large crew. The big cutter was ten times the size of any of Downey's boats that he'd helmed. *Chase*'s motto now took on a personal meaning.

Downey immersed himself in work, listening, watching, reading and asking about anything he did not fully understand. As always, he contributed more than he took. All the while, Downey managed the ship's complement of boatswain's mates, acted as junior deck watch officer on the bridge, as assistant boarding officer during safety at sea inspections and as junior officer of the deck in port.

Soon after arriving, Downey's thriving imprint as COB was visible to others. The ship's captain noted in official correspondence that "Chief Downey's action saved *Chase* and her crew from serious material and physical harm in July of 1982. While practicing an emergency breakaway during an underway replenishment, the ship experienced a power surge which prematurely parted the fuel line spewing fuel oil over the decks and parting the tending and communication lines. The only line that was holding, but dangerously close to parting, was the span wire. Realizing the danger of the span wire parting and probably whipping across the decks, Downey assisted by BM2 Brian Marks, placed their own safety aside, muscling the pelican hook free, thereby disconnecting the span wire, and eliminating danger."[25]

Chief Downey made a difference on *Chase*, both operationally and among the deck gang members he led. During a reenlistment counseling session with twenty-two-year-old BM2 Marks, Marks had the notion to become a commercial fisherman. He was about to experience a life-altering lesson—one that was both harsh and instructive. "Downey asked me what I was going to do when I got out, and I mentioned I was hoping to get on a fishing trawler so I could continue working on the water. He smiled and told me he could help me get on a boat since he knew some trawler captains, and he could give me an idea of what life would be like. I was thrilled to get the help, and really impressed that he would help me even though I was getting out. After the workday, and while we were on duty in port we met on the fantail. He stood next to a garbage can from the galley full of the day's trash and asked me if I still wanted the training, I said yes. Right then, he took the garbage can and dumped it on the deck and kicked the pile around."[26]

Downey's dose of simple wisdom continued, with Marks recollecting, "The Chief told me to not just pick up the garbage, but to put the plastic in one pile, paper in another, cardboard in a third, etc., until I had piles of assorted trash all over the deck. He then gave me a ruler and told me to measure each piece of trash and sort it by size. This whole time I was getting madder and madder at him, but this was the old Guard and a BM2 never argued with the Chief, period. After sorting the trash, Chief Downey had me put all the little piles back in the trash can and clean the deck. He then asked me if I enjoyed sorting the trash…and being a bit upset, I said it wasn't that bad in a sarcastic but respectful way. He laughed and said working on a fishing boat is just like what you just did, dumping stuff on deck, separating it, then sorting by size and throwing most of it back in the sea…for 12 hours at a time….He then left the fantail…while I fumed."[27]

A few weeks later, Chief Downey asked Marks if there was a job in the Coast Guard he really wanted and where he wanted to go. Marks mentioned that his only regret after four years was not qualifying as a 44-motor lifeboat (MLB) coxswain at a lifeboat station. Without telling Marks, Downey contacted the detailer—an assigner of posts—and worked a deal to get him a lifeboat station billet in Ocean City, Maryland. The rest was history.

Marks sailed to Europe on *Chase*, with Chief Downey "giving me some great responsibilities and advice along the way. During slow periods, he drilled me on navigation rules of the road and the contents of a reference book on the MLBs. Once I left *Chase*, I went to Ocean City and qualified Heavy Weather Coxswain and kept in touch with the Chief for several years."[28] Eventually, Marks retired as a senior chief boatswain after serving as an OIC of the MLB station in Hatteras, North Carolina, and accumulating eight years at sea. "Without Chief Downey's fantail training and his gentle prodding of my detailer in 1982, who knows what would have happened but, in my eyes, he did a great thing. I still have my old CG 313 [boat crew qualification manual] signed by him."[29]

In late October 1983, a *Chase* junior officer led a boarding team onto the eighty-five-foot motor vessel *Black Hawk*, a coastal freighter smuggling bulk marijuana to the United States. The vessel was spotted by a maritime patrol aircraft, and *Chase* was sent to find it. The intercept occurred four hundred nautical miles northeast of Puerto Rico. The vessel gave *Chase*'s team consent to board to verify its nationality because the master claimed it was Colombian, but it was documented as Panamanian. The homeport painted on the stern was also Panamanian.

The vessel was assimilated "stateless" through a Coast Guard process called "Statement of No Objection," and an order was issued to seize the vessel and arrest the six Colombians onboard. The smell of marijuana was overwhelming—the *Black Hawk* had more than five hundred bales on board weighing more than twenty-nine thousand pounds total.

After the crew was arrested and the vessel seized, the boarding team was swapped out for a custody crew. One person from the original boarding team remained to ensure the "chain of custody" of the evidence until the vessel reached San Juan. The *Black Hawk*'s new Coast Guard crew was to sail independently to San Juan and navigate and keep the prize vessel afloat as it was taking on water. *Chase* ended up escorting the smuggling vessel on its four-day trip because *Black Hawk* had no food or water.

None of the makeshift crew had driven an eighty-five-foot fishing vessel before, but Jack Downey had plenty of experience driving smaller boats, including fishing boats. He could have easily driven the *Black Hawk* himself, but instead, he made the trip a series of teaching moments and coached his prize crew. Each time they drove alongside *Chase* to hook up a sea painter and reprovision, a new prize crew member would learn a new skill under his watchful eye. While not technically in command of the vessel, he made sure that the seized boat arrived safely in San Juan.[30]

One officer who served with Downey on *Chase* said of him, "He had a way of teaching you to develop a skill while preventing the panic that often accompanies learning operational skills. He seemed happy when his 'students' learned and matured and had a way of instilling a sense of pride in the student for learning a difficult skill."[31]

During his assignment on *Chase*, Downey dished out lessons on shore as well as underway. When Downey was on the *Chase*'s quarterdeck as junior officer of the deck in port, several crewmen came up the gangway, late from liberty. These were repeat offenders, and Jack soon appeared with a pair of scissors; the OOD looked on, puzzled. A few hours later, the chief and the OOD talked about what to do with the crewmen late from liberty. Downey said, "I've got it covered, Lieutenant." Downey then used the scissors to cut up the late arrivers' ID cards. He told them they could go back on liberty as soon as they got new ID cards. Little did they know that Downey had made a phone call to the chief yeoman who oversaw the issuance of IDs and asked him to not be available for three days. In hindsight, it was an elegant solution. None would receive adverse "paper" for their misconduct and none of their careers were impacted, but they all learned a valuable lesson.[32]

As Chief Downey's notoriety grew on *Chase* and throughout New England's Chief's Petty Officer's Association, a referral from Chief Downey was as good as gold, increasing the odds that whomever he was calling for was up to the task and would succeed.

In the winter of 1982–83, *Chase* was assigned to take station off the South American coast to determine how many potential drug vessels might be headed north. During this deployment, a boarding was attempted on a medium-sized, poorly maintained freighter with a history of transporting marijuana. While making ready to lower the motor surf boat (MSB) with the boarding party, the freighter attempted to ram *Chase*. The freighter had radioed that her engines had failed, but she still was moving forward toward *Chase*.

The MSB was hanging over *Chase*'s side with boat crew and boarding party onboard. The deck crew was waiting for the bridge command to lower away the MSB. In an instant, the freighter was ten yards away from *Chase* and getting closer and was going to ram the cutter. The boat officer ordered everyone out of the MSB, but the crew was confused. They were unhappy about the turmoil after a long search to find the freighter. Chief Downey immediately keyed in on the officer's order, instantly recognizing the freighter's "closing" position. Standing in the MSB and closer to *Chase*'s rail, he started physically lifting members out of the boat, yelling at them to get to *Chase*'s starboard side. It didn't take more than a few members to be jettisoned before everyone understood the concern, and the small boat was soon empty.

The boat crew didn't say five words throughout the entire evolution. Had the freighter been going faster or been any closer, the MSB would have been torn away and its crew with it. Later, the crew was told that *Chase*'s CO had taken control of the cutter when he saw the freighter's angle change. By quickly giving several helm and engine commands in rapid succession, *Chase* avoided a catastrophe.

Downey's only comment was, "That was kinda close," just as general quarters sounded.

Chapter 4

CLOSER TO HOME

Between 1984 and 1987, Downey accepted assignments on shore and afloat. He departed cutter *Chase* and reported to Station Woods Hole as the officer in charge in 1984. Station Woods Hole was co-located with Group Woods Hole, the regional parent command for fifteen stations and cutters. This brought him back to home waters, closer to family.

Woods Hole—a wee village—crackles with vigor and energy. Just outside the Coast Guard station gate is a compact, traditional New England "Main Street" replete with restaurants, cafés, ice cream shops and gift shops, designed for tourists using nearby ferries for Martha's Vineyard and Nantucket. A small drawbridge that halts busy summer vehicle traffic allows small boats to enter Eel Pond, providing safe harbor from nearby Woods Hole Passage. The Woods Hole Oceanographic Institution and Marine Biological Laboratory buildings and piers are also within a quarter mile.

Wherever Downey was stationed, he worked to make the station part of the community it served. This time around, what worried Downey was just a half mile to the west near the ferry piers, the treacherous Woods Hole Passage, a narrow channel connecting Buzzards Bay to Vineyard Sound, was a constant threat. On either side of the one-hundred-yard-wide channel were fierce currents, rocky ledges and dangerous shoals marked by buoys. Any inexperienced mariner would be intimidated.

Downey facetiously thought that "port and starboard guard rails" installed so that boats could "just pinball between the rails" instead of going aground would be the safest and smartest thing to do. This was especially true for sailboats, which usually did not have engines large enough to overpower the currents or to avoid a shoal while being swept along rapidly. He knew that few boaters had the patience to wait for a slack tide when there was less risk.

Downey's time at Station Woods Hole was productive. The station's crews responded to more than eight hundred distress calls, saving forty-five lives, assisting two thousand mariners and salvaging property valued at more than $25 million.[33]

Most notable was Downey's "calming influence" during a rescue of passengers and crew from the coastal cruise ship *Pilgrim Belle*, which struck a submerged rock off Cuttyhunk Island in July 1985 and began to sink with 108 elderly passengers. Once the mayday came in, Downey ordered station boats and requested additional nearby civilian vessels to assist. His quick response averted panic onboard.[34]

One month later in August 1985, Downey displayed "exceptional competence and bravery" in leading the station crews in the rescue of nine crew members in peril by a raging engine room fire onboard the fishing vessel *Nordic Pride*.[35]

In June 1987, Downey was credited as a proactive partner by harbormasters, commercial salvors and the boating public, including educating them on the need for safety and law enforcement boardings. He also promoted the Coast Guard's image by undertaking extensive boat and communication training with the local Coast Guard Auxiliary branch.[36]

His work with the commercial salvage operators became the model for how Coast Guard commands interacted with salvors in 1988, when the government sponsored legislation to share rescue responsibilities in assisting mariners in trouble. Downey was frequently called on to be the interface with testy salvors during the transition to shared procedures and calibrating policy that determined if, when and how private sector rescue entities would take on or give up cases.

It was during Downey's assignment to Station Woods Hole that he met the first of three protégés who would stand on his shoulders for many years to come, and this person would be one of several acolytes who would eventually carry Downey's coffin in 2022. Seaman Gordon McClay met Downey in 1986 at Station Woods Hole. "Gordie" had joined the Coast Guard in 1983 and lived in a coastal town south of Boston, so the Coast Guard was familiar to him—so familiar that after graduating from high school, he had pretty much settled on joining the Guard.[37]

McClay was stationed aboard the eighty-two-foot-long, multi-mission cutter *Point Bonita* (WPM 82347), moored at the Station Woods Hole pier.

After "striking" boatswain's mate on the cutter (striking refers to when a seaman or non-rate aspires for a particular specialty rating and spends extra time becoming familiar with the craft), McClay was assigned to Station Woods Hole and introduced himself to Downey. McClay broke in as a coxswain (the person in charge of a boat) under Downey. McClay was flabbergasted that Downey spent literally hundreds of hours underway with him and other crew members. McClay's certification board was two days long, not including an additional fourteen hours of questioning at the station. The qualification board was so lengthy and complete that McClay remembers the details as if it were yesterday, grousing that significant events can have that affect. He avowed that those numbers of hours were neither exaggerated nor embellished. Yet McClay's time with Downey at Station Woods Hole became the foundation that brought McClay to be the Coast Guard leader he was meant to be.[38]

In the summer of 1987, Downey transferred to be the officer in charge of the sixty-five-foot cutter *Towline*, moored in Bristol, Rhode Island. Bristol is a classic New England deepwater seaport with historic roots. Its principal businesses were marine related and tourism, hosting great seafood restaurants, diverse antique stores and unique haberdasheries. Located on the east side of Narragansett Bay, "America's most patriotic town" boasts of the oldest Fourth of July Parade and the famous Herreshoff Marine Museum. Working aboard the *Towline*, a small and squat harbor tug with a crew of five, was Downey's dream job. The station was closer to Downey's home than Woods Hole, and it had a small crew and a single diesel engine. *Towline* wasn't fast, but she was sturdy, built for breaking winter ice and servicing aids to navigation.

Ice breaking was especially important for heating fuel/oil deliveries to many New England ports, including the islands of Nantucket and Martha's Vineyard during cold winter months. Few remember that the large swath of the ocean regularly froze over prior to today's publicity of climate change, severely affecting the commerce and energy needs of remote islands. One of Downey's greatest joys was when he broke ice just a short distance away in Greenwich Bay, spanning an area near Warwick to East Greenwich, Rhode Island. Downey's parents lived in an apartment overlooking the bay, and his elderly father never failed to mention when he saw the tug "bellying up on a sheet of ice to snap it away and open up the cove for the quahoggers to get out."

Considering how much Downey liked the harbor tug duty, the crew and being home with Judith and his family, the year passed quickly. He was promoted to senior chief boatswain's mate in the active duty and hadn't thought about looking for a new billet; he thought he'd wait until January to contact his detailer.

In November 1988, as Downey got cutter *Towline* ready for the ice breaking season, a longtime friend called. Captain Fred Hamilton, now commander of Group Woods Hole, asked Downey to take charge of Station Chatham. Downey and Captain Hamilton had served on the cutter *Chase* four years earlier, where Hamilton was a commander and the executive officer and Downey was chief of the boat. Recent troubles at Station Chatham included a failed rescue of a fishing boat on Chatham Bar. Downey was needed as soon as possible. Several scathing newspaper articles and a town hall meeting demanded that the officer in charge be relieved. It was time for Chief "Fix-It" to do what he did best, again.

Chapter 5

PIONEERING COMMERCIAL AND COAST GUARD SMALL BOAT SAFETY

When Downey reported to Station Chatham, the weather had been reasonable, slowly evolving into a typical Cape Cod winter. He initially inspected the small boats and found a forty-one-foot utility boat and a forty-four-foot motor lifeboat in their cradles in the station's parking lot. Downey intended to get the boats back in the water ASAP and make the station the best in the Coast Guard.

Chatham is renowned in Coast Guard circles. Downey knew the rip currents throughout Nantucket Sound but especially near Monomoy, which is a National Wildlife Refuge and attracts more than piping plovers—it had become a refuge for seals that attracted a population of great white sharks and tourists. He also knew that in the blink of an eye on a sunny day, the weather could change to pea soup fog, "socking in" tourists fishing for stripers. When this happened, panicked anglers called for help.

To help during this transition on Cape Cod's southern elbow, Downey privately cornered his executive petty officer, BM2 Tom Guthlein. Downey explained to Guthlein that he knew small boats, but not necessarily shallow-water surf boats, and navigating the treacherous Chatham Bar. Downey told Guthlein that he wanted Guthlein to teach him everything he knew so that Downey could get the crew uniformly trained and the station working at maximum output, without delay.

The young second-class boatswain's mate was quiet, reserved and respectful, but more importantly, he was squared away. Guthlein had reported to Station Chatham several months before Downey following a three-year posting at Station Merrimac River, a motor lifeboat surf station on the border of New Hampshire and Massachusetts. That Guthlein had earned his heavy weather coxswain and surfman qualifications at Station Merrimac River impressed Downey. Guthlein was also a qualified coxswain on both the forty-one-foot and forty-four-foot small boats, as well as heavy weather qualified; he wore his surfman pin with pride.

Downey ordered Guthlein that Station Chatham needed a "stand down," meaning no active or reserve crew could take a boat out for SAR or training without Downey's approval. Research would also be conducted to determine if other types of boats were more suitable for the shallow water Chatham Bar surf conditions, as well as new types of cold weather personal protective equipment.

For the next eighteen months, Downey pushed his crews. Many rejected Downey's "tear down and build back up" philosophy. Some decided that his corrective actions were "overboard" and demeaning and requested transfers. Others persevered, acknowledging that Downey's leadership was not easy on the crew but that everyone was treated the same without exception.

Downey and some crew members in work blues pose in front of Chatham Light with breaches buoy and Lyle guns, circa 1998. *CWO Guthlein.*

During the five years that Downey served as the officer in charge of Station Chatham, he transformed the crew and station. Downey tested prototype waterjet-driven twenty-eight-foot LeCompte boats for shallow-water surf and bar conditions. He ordered and conducted detailed evaluations leading to operational models that remain the standard, even at some of today's small boat stations and cutters.

The master chief's crews began wearing dry suits, spearheading a new lifesaving national doctrine. Downey reestablished a surf qualification program ensuring that crews were ready to respond in all weather conditions. He trained them in all types of weather and surf conditions. Downey gave the title of "Surfman" a new meaning. It was not only a qualification but also a level of expertise, linking the Coast Guard's past lifesaving history to modern times. And Downey rebuilt a strong relationship with the town and its fishing community by establishing the New England's Commercial Fishing Vessel Safety Seminar, today commonplace throughout the Coast Guard.

As June 1990 arrived, the boats were back in the water, and many were recertified. As a testament to his performance, Downey's supervisors nominated him for the U.S. Navy League's coveted Douglas A. Munro Award for inspirational leadership. Signalman Douglas Munro is the only Coast Guardsman to have received the Congressional Medal of Honor. Munro received his award posthumously after rescuing U.S. marines from the 7th Battalion on September 27, 1942, off Guadalcanal. Munro died at the age of twenty-two when a .30-caliber Japanese round pierced his skull as he piloted his Higgins boat and the marines back to safety.

Each year, the Navy League awards the Douglas A. Munro Inspirational Leadership Award to the Coast Guard enlisted member who has demonstrated outstanding leadership and professional competence to the extent of their rank and rate. Criteria for the award, which Downey eventually received, includes:

- Consistently demonstrate outstanding leadership skills which motivate and inspire personnel to strive for excellence and achieve measurable results that contribute to the success of the Coast Guard.
- Possess the ability to create and maintain a positive culture where the differences of all personnel are respected so that all can achieve their full potential and maximize their contributions to Coast Guard missions.

- Act with strategic intent to ensure optimization of resources, influence the success of major operations or programs and achieve operational excellence.
- Guided, coached or mentored others to reach new levels of performance.[39]

BM3 Sheila Lucey's experience exemplified the transformative power of Downey's leadership. She reported to Station Chatham in August 1990. "I immediately learned that I WAS NOT even close to being ready to be certified as a surfman. I wasn't ready for the pace; the billion questions about everything; being challenged about everything; being challenged even if I was right…having to tell him how come I was right and how come I knew/thought I was right," Lucey remembered. "I was not ready for having someone that knew what I was thinking before I even knew what I was thinking and that absolutely did not buy one single thing that I was selling. He constantly challenged us. You always knew where you stood with him. He was confident but not arrogant with a quick wit and an overabundance of common sense."[40]

Downey continued to build his own expertise by attending the National Motor Lifeboat School at Cape Disappointment, Washington, in January 1991. During a training session, he witnessed the sinking of the F/V *Sea King*, a stern trawler whose crew called for assistance. Downey's boat was not far from the breaking bar and the foundering vessel. The trawler needed to be towed across the bar. As preparations were made, the vessel capsized. Five people drowned—three crew members from the fishing vessel, their skipper and one Coast Guard medic. Several months later, in May 1991, Downey received his surfman certificate, no. 206, and the station acquired a new twenty-eight-foot LeCompte, a much-needed experimental shallow-water surf boat.

Senior Chief Lucey with her mentors: *Pendleton* rescue hero Bernie Webber and Downey at Station Chatham, circa 1990. *Authors' collection.*

Downey worked the LeCompte in all types of sea conditions and included himself as crew. Overall, he was satisfied with the boat's performance. He saw it becoming a principal platform at Chatham and other stations, like Ocean City or even Hatteras, and on small and large cutters. He solicited feedback from crew members and told his executive petty officer, Tom Guthlein, that once the boating season was over and the weather got frosty, he'd like to take a ride, maybe to Nantucket, to test the boat's comfortability and functionality of the new full-length dry suits in which they'd been training.

Downey couldn't wait that long. He'd worked for two years to get the twenty-eight-foot LeCompte and was eager to take it for a long run. Why wait until early winter? He decided to leave on the next good weather day. Word spread quickly, and a small crowd filed down to Station Nantucket's newly constructed docks to see the arrival of the prototype boat. It was an early spring day, and in the distance, you could hear a fast-moving vessel coming down the channel. Then suddenly it appeared from around Brant Point Light at a high rate of speed.

The boat made a sharp turn toward the dock at Station Brant Point and sped past the dock. Downey, the coxswain, put the jet boat's helm over hard left. On waterjet-driven boats, that response is immediate, unlike a conventionally powered small craft. Downey and the boat jackknifed and immediately came about 180 degrees at well over twenty-five knots, propelling the second crewman like a skipping flat rock in the opposite direction, also at twenty-five knots.

Those observing saw this impressive demonstration of speed and maneuverability, while others simply saw a crewman ejected. Downey realized that he'd launched his crewman and turned to retrieve him; then he sheepishly made for the Station Brant Point's dock. Somehow, he made it a teachable moment, articulating, "And that's why we wear our safety harnesses in these things!"

High Winds

Hurricane Bob soon gave the station extra work in August 1991. A hurricane in the Chatham area is especially lethal because the coastline is mainly low-lying beaches, which do not offer protection from the destructive winds and crashing Atlantic surf. Property damage is usually high, and saltwater inlets leading to hidden bays were altered; many of these waterways became dangerous and unusable. More hurricanes came after Bob in quick succession.

In late October, a second hurricane hit the Chatham coast. Dubbed the "Halloween Hurricane," its might was destructive on land and at sea, and it earned the nickname the "Perfect Storm." Power throughout Chatham was out, and roads were flooded. Trees and power poles were down, blocking roads and making repairs nearly impossible. The station and lighthouse ran on generators.

Many commercial boats and floating docks had broken free. Station crews went from marina to marina trying to minimize damage by securing loose fishing and pleasure boats and docks. Downey and Guthlein checked on the new LeCompte. After they snared a fishing boat that broke free from its mooring, they spotted the LeCompte. It was still secured to its dock, the view obscured by a fishing boat that had broken free and was pressed against the LeCompte, chafing its inflatable hull with every choppy wave and gust of wind. Downey quipped, "That's a $150,000 fender that guy is using…we better get to it."[41]

Downey spent that winter planning a fishing vessel safety seminar. In the spring, Downey hosted New England's first Commercial Fishing Vessel Safety Symposium. "Chief Downey was a blessing to Chatham. A real spark to the entire community. He turned the whole station around, the fishing community and town regarding their belief in the Coast Guard," recalled Ernest Eldridge of the Chatham branch of the Cape Cod Fishery Alliance. Long days and nights of training would continue to be tested by real-world events.

Other Adventures

At 9:28 p.m. on August 7, 1992, the *Queen Elizabeth II* ocean liner grounded two and a half miles south of Cuttyhunk Island en route to New York City. Captain Robin Allen Woodall was pushing the liner's 130,000-horsepower diesel electric engines to make up for delays as the vessel weighed anchor near East Chop on Martha's Vineyard. The liner suffered extensive hull damage as the vessel "squatted" down and struck uncharted boulders while moving near her top speed of thirty-four knots. The passengers were evacuated and transported to Newport on every available Coast Guard, harbormaster and civilian vessel that could assist. The *Queen Elizabeth II* was towed to Boston for repairs in drydock.[42]

In May 1993, at Downey's change of command, hundreds of people from the Chatham area attended, honoring him for his dedication and service to the Coast Guard and the community. The town showed its thanks with testimonials and proclamations. The fishing community was so grateful that there was standing room only on the station's lawn. During his years managing Station Chatham, he was credited with "his crews responding to

Coast Guard Station Brant Point, Nantucket. *Brian Tague.*

400 law enforcement boardings, nearly 800 search and rescue cases involving more than 1,400 mariners with 40 lives saved, while displaying exceptional leadership and competence."[43]

After receiving his award, Downey calmly took the podium and politely gave thanks while simultaneously motioning to the station's crew standing at attention behind him, stating, "The credit goes to them, not me." Democratic Congressman Gerry Studds read a Commonwealth of Massachusetts's proclamation extolling Downey's contributions to Cape Cod's constituents, particularly the fishing community and the town of Chatham.

When Downey departed Station Chatham in 1993, he was an acknowledged expert in small and surf boat operations, redefining the meaning of "Surfman." His next mission was Station Brant Point on Nantucket, which further tested Downey's skill sets in those iconic and renowned but treacherous waters.

Chapter 6

LATER YEARS AND SERVICE CHALLENGES

After Downey's change of command in Chatham, the Downey family took a ferry ride to their new home on Nantucket. Nantucket, or the "Grey Lady" as ancient mariners lovingly referred to the island because of the thick shrouds of fog that sometimes blanketed the area in the early morning and evening, lies just twenty miles south of Chatham, separated by Nantucket Sound, with Monomoy Island and Shoals guarding its entrance from the open Atlantic.

Downey was in the right location professionally, but as a family man, his own family's happiness was uppermost in his mind. Would they acclimate to a new move to Nantucket? After all, they'd been in Cape Cod Air Station government housing since 1984, when Downey was officer in charge at Station Woods Hole.

In the ten years since, Judith and the children other than Jennifer, who had gone out on her own in 1988, had carved themselves a slice of Cape Cod happiness. Judith made friends and enjoyed working part time on Cape Cod. And the kids made more friends than they ever could in Narraganset, often playing outside until well after dark. For the four children affected by the move, from ages fourteen to twenty, Downey had a gnawing concern about them making new friends. Unlike at the quarters at Cape Cod, which was a stone's throw from Hyannis and Plymouth, traveling on and off Nantucket took advance planning and patience for weather allowances. It was "island life," with its unique challenges and opportunities. But in no time, Downey became familiar with the island and his new command, and Judith made their new house a home. The kids navigated the new school and made friends.

By the following spring, Station Brant Point had simmered down, but more change was afoot as Downey's executive petty officer (XPO) was promoted and transferred. Downey needed to replace him, and BM1 Gordie McClay recalled, "Downey called and asks me if I would be interested in joining him at Brant Point as XPO on Nantucket. I was very interested but had concerns. I owned a home in Plymouth and was skeptical of moving and going to the island. I countered asking Downey if he would consider if I could be a 'geographical bachelor.' Downey declined, saying being a geographical bachelor in a command position on the island will not work."

Downey convinced McClay to bring his family for a short visit. After a day with the Downeys, the McClay clan made the decision to accept the orders to Nantucket. "I will never forget or ever regret that decision. That tour with Senior Chief Downey absolutely solidified my desire to be a leader in the U.S. Coast Guard and pursue the organization's highest qualification for an enlisted person in charge," said McClay. And they had a little fun along the way, hanging out with their families, fishing, scalloping and seeing all that Nantucket offered during McClay's tour of duty from April 1994 to May 1997.

Downey and McClay had previously worked together on the famous CG36500 when they were both at Chatham, and they mustered the troops about a project to further preserve the historic 1952 rescue boat and a U.S. Life-Saving Service pulling boat. The crew agreed and spent hundreds of hours fixing and getting the iconic boats seaworthy and transitioned them from museum pieces to treasured artifacts in near-perfect condition. They raced the pulling boat from the harbor entrance to the Coast Guard docks.

"There were hundreds, if not thousands, of people watching this race. To practice we would row around using Coast Guard book Number One

Opposite: Downey off Brant Point, Nantucket, at the tiller of a U.S. Life-Saving Service pulling boat, overlooking the iconic CG36500 rescue boat, a forty-four-foot MLB and the forty-seven-foot MLB, collectively representing one hundred years of history. *Brian Tague.*

Left: Master Chief Downey commands a Race Point surfboat for the Nantucket races, summer of 1994 (a gathering of a century of surfboats). *Brian Tague.*

commands in learning how they did it 'back in the day.' We took the motor lifeboat standardization team out for a row when we had our stan team visit and they were impressed. It was one of the coolest things I have done in the Coast Guard. The teamwork and volunteerism to accomplish this was outstanding. Downey, Senior Chief at the time, was instrumental in putting this together."[44]

Retired Navy Commander Maurice Gibbs, a longtime friend of the Coast Guard and Nantucket fixture, felt that Downey and his crew's work was worthy of acknowledgment and wrote to his museum's board: "And speaking of great work, the entire crew under the direction of Senior Chief Jack Downey has fully restored the Beach Cart. It has been put through its paces at the Harbor Fest, and the Country Fair. The Coast Guardsmen have picked up the techniques from their forefathers like real pros! Other recognition…Jack Downey (again) and his new XPO Gordon McClay who moved the Race Point Lifeboat outside and spent nearly the entire day scrubbing it down. It looks like new. That is the kind of spirit that keeps the museum going."[45]

It is also the kind of spirit that Downey instilled in his crews. The Brant Point Light would soon have a new wreath with crossed oars for the Christmas holiday season. The U.S. Life-Saving Service Lyle gun would sound over the harbor, startling unknowing tourists. The breeches buoy would be exercised, with station volunteers taking the seat. The Nantucket Senior Center's Valentine's Day dance would be manned by clumsy station crew members, and watching Friday night football was another big part of station life. Crew members were constantly challenged but never wanted to disappoint Senior Chief Downey whenever he called on them.

On June 10, 1995, the Panamanian cruise ship *Royal Majesty* ran aground while returning from Bermuda en route to Boston. She bottomed out on the Rose and Crown Shoal, ten miles east of Nantucket. This location was seventeen miles from where the watch officers thought they were. Poor watch keeping and a global positioning system (GPS) failure were to blame. A wire had come loose on the ship's GPS, and the liner had stopped receiving precision satellite fixes. Harsh sea conditions and inclement weather initially prevented the removal of its 1,509 passengers. Downey's rescue boats stood by, and a radio watch was maintained. With the assistance of five tugs, the cruise ship was pulled free and returned to Boston the next day without incident. Damage to the vessel and lost revenue totaled $7 million.[46] Downey quipped, "They got lucky."

Changes Afoot

Downey trained the Brant Point crew into a fine-tuned machine. He enjoyed the station's solid reputation and family life on the island. He wanted to do more but hesitated when his XPO, BM1 McClay, received orders to transfer. Downey recognized that it was a positive move for McClay's long-term career, but nonetheless he was sorry to see him go.

Downey also concurrently took command of another unit, this time aboard the cutter *Point Hannon*, an eighty-two-foot patrol boat homeported in Maine, from December 1997 to February 1998. The cutter's OIC was determined to be temporarily medically unfit for sea duty. It took Downey only twelve days to get acclimated on the new state-of-the-art cutter, and he immediately filled a key operational role as the Gulf of Maine search and rescue cutter. In three months, the vessel logged "202 underway hours, including three law enforcement operations, one SAR case, thirteen boardings, resulting in four fishery violations and six commercial fishing safety violations, ending with two weeks of dockside maintenance."[47] Downey was commended by the Southwest Harbor Group commander for his dedication, personal sacrifice and outstanding performance of duty.[48]

As winter turned into spring, Downey realized that in just a few short months, he'd be headed back to Station Point Judith in Rhode Island. He was happy that he'd again take command of his "second home." But he was also melancholy. Unlike when the family first arrived at Nantucket five years earlier, Jack and Judy would be heading back to the Downey family home in Rhode Island alone as "empty nesters." Their kids, now adults, were either working and on their own or out of state in college.

At Downey's change of command on Nantucket, he received a second commendation medal for his five-year tenure from May 1993 to June 1998. Under his direction, he successfully oversaw six hundred SAR cases and more than five hundred law enforcement boardings, exhibiting outstanding knowledge and unsurpassed communication skills. He demonstrated excellent risk assessment during a difficult and pressing rescue of the F/V *Sea Lion*, rescuing all personnel just minutes before the vessel sank. He also voluntarily assumed a concurrent OIC position with short notice aboard the *Point Hannon* of Maine, excelling in patrol boat operations during harsh winter conditions.

A Promotion

Back at Station Point Judith in September 1998, Downey received a promotion to master chief. The first year was typical for the newly promoted master chief. He assessed the readiness of the unit, made improvements where needed, held the line and reached out to the community. As the summer of 1999 approached, Downey made ready for a busy season, focusing on the days between the Fourth of July and Labor Day. It was crunch time for pleasure boaters, along with the ferry service heading to Block Island and the charter fishing boats working out of several nearby ports, including Newport, Jamestown and Galilee.

But two weeks after the Fourth of July, all bets were off. He and the station's crews ramped up for a life-changing event during which they'd play a pivotal role, hours upon end. In the late evening of July16, a private single-prop Piper Saratoga plane went missing. Its occupants were JFK Jr.; his wife, Carolyn Bessette; and her sister, Lauren Bessette. The flight, with Kennedy at the controls, originated from the Caldwell, New Jersey airport with a visual flight rule flight path along the Connecticut coast, crossing Rhode Island Sound and scheduled to land at Martha's Vineyard. The plane never arrived. The Coast Guard at Group Woods Hole was called early the following morning, and the service coordinated a search using aircraft, small boats and cutters from multiple agencies. There was intense media coverage and scrutiny.

Downey knew the waters well. He estimated a general area to search using the tide, currents and the last known radar location of the plane from the Federal Aviation Administration. Debris was found in the waters south of Martha's Vineyard about seven miles short of the plane's desired runway.[49] Downey's unit was among the thirty-odd commands from twenty different agencies that searched for and eventually recovered the victims' bodies seven and a quarter miles southwest of Martha's Vineyard.

He was the first Coast Guard operational commander to recognize that other units needed to search the approaches to the Martha's Vineyard airport. The three victims and their aircraft were first detected by NOAA side scanning sonar, and the bodies and the plane were quickly recovered by U.S. Navy divers. The ashes of the deceased were later ceremoniously placed on the seas at the exact location of the crash. The National Transportation Safety Board (NTSB) report would go on to indicate that the pilot, traveling in near darkness without his flight instructor, had become spatially disoriented.

One Long Summer and Fall

Downey took temporary and concurrent command of another eighty-seven-foot patrol boat, this one based out of nearby Woods Hole, the cutter *Hammerhead*, for three months when the skipper fell down a ladder and broke his leg. Then, just three and half months after the JFK Jr. crash, on Halloween 1999, EgyptAir 990, a commercial airliner with 217 passengers and crew onboard, plummeted into the Atlantic Ocean sixty miles south of Nantucket. Downey worked the scene of the crash area with cutter *Hammerhead* from October 31 to November 7. The leadership and superb management skills demonstrated by Coast Guard units and personnel were crucial to the full-scale recovery effort. After the tragedy, Downey, true to

Coast Guard cutter *Hammerhead* off Station Point Judith. *Brian Tague.*

form, made cold weather recommendations for the new eighty-seven-foot Marine Protector–class cutter based on his crew's experiences.[50]

As Downey settled into the new year at Station Point Judith for what would be a short tenure, he was again transferred back to Station Brant Point as a temporary and concurrent officer in charge when the skipper in Nantucket was sent off island to joint service training at the Coast Guard Academy in New London. At Downey's change of command from his "second home" at Station Point Judith, he received his third commendation medal for his tenure from June 1998 to July 2000. His multiple outstanding achievements while serving as OIC of Station Point Judith include temporarily and concurrently acting as OIC of Station's Block Island (small), Brant Point, LORAN Station Nantucket and *Hammerhead*; prosecuting several high-profile search and rescue cases, including JFK Jr.'s plane crash and the Black Point fishermen search; and serving on a 2001 commandant-ordered Marine Investigation Board for the deaths of two Guardsmen at Station Niagara, New York, where he made sound recommendations for their safe operational use on all CG cutters following a capsizing.[51]

Before Downey departed from Point Judith, his XPO conveyed the crew's sentiments in a letter. The letter was the quintessential response after a tour with Downey:

> *Master Chief, we would like to express our appreciation for teaching us and setting the benchmark which is second to none. When you first came to the Station, our vision was cloudy at best. Slowly you tuned us in and today we must say that everything is crystal clear. Don't get us wrong there were many bumps in the road and at some time or another, we all wanted to quit, but somehow you pulled us back in and we thank you for that. Anybody worth their salt can look past an ass chewing and understand it was the right thing to do and, in the end, you made us a stronger and more professional crew. What you taught us cannot be measured and we will carry it with us for life. Learning from you is equivalent to combat experience, anything else is just a training mission. Today is truly a sad day, we feel a piece of history is walking out the front door before its time. We are truly honored to be a part of the Master Chief Downey legend and to have served alongside of you. We are sure your name will live forever through the kids and grandkids of those who had the pleasure to serve with you. Master Chief, the crew of Station Point Judith salutes you and wishes you continued success in your future endeavors. If there is anything we can do for you, it would be our pleasure and we would do it with pride, just as you have taught us.*[52]

Downey's next assignment might have been his most difficult. He was to teach future enlisted and officer leaders at the Coast Guard Academy. For most of his career, he had been "operational" in the field of seas, leading and managing from the front lines. Now he would be carrying a briefcase and teaching and instructing from behind a desk and a lectern. What could go wrong?

Chapter 7

"DOWNEY-ISMS" FROM THE FACTORY

Other than being underway aboard cutters on patrol, Master Chief Downey hadn't been assigned any farther south than the 02882 zip code of his Point Judith homestead. During his seven previous permanent officer in charge assignments, he rotated between afloat and ashore units and multiple and sometimes dizzying repeat tours in Chatham, Woods Hole, on Nantucket and Point Judith. In at least two shore station assignments, he spent five years each at stations Chatham and Nantucket. Those assignments were operational. No sand had made its way into this man's polished military shoes, just salt.

But the enlisted detailer—who doles out assignments—had other ideas for Downey. The terse government assignment message commanded the master chief to head south and west to the Coast Guard Academy to instruct at the Command and Operations school on the neatly manicured 103-acre campus. According to government records at the time, "Command and Operations prepares personnel to serve in senior operational, leadership and command positions aboard all classes of cutters and at operational units ashore."[53]

Downey became acclimated and taught portions of six separate courses at the Academy's Leadership Development Center (LDC). The LDC was established in 1998 and subsumed the Command and Operations School formal content as well as his simple wisdom to students ranging from second class (E5) petty officers to captains (O6) and senior leaders, both from the United States and foreign maritime agencies.

The position the master chief would fill was important for several reasons. Since the addition of his billet in Command and Operations School in 1997, Coast Guard Headquarters had made at least one attempt to reclaim the position and use it elsewhere. However, the Academy superintendent fended off the raid on Downey's position, rationalizing that the addition of the E9 position "had enabled the school staff to produce three additional courses per year, totaling eight class convenings. Prior to the addition of the E9 position, classes had to be smaller, numerous waivers had to be granted and many (Executive Petty Officers) XPOs and (Officers in Charge) OICs never attended the school. If the BMCM billet is removed in FY00, the School staff would be forced to return to the previous course loading, and cancel the prospective operations officer course, the (Team Coordination Training) TCT courses and the (International Maritime Operations Course) IMOC courses."[54]

For the first time in his career, the master chief felt like a duck out of water, literally. He did everything he could to delay the inevitable. Soon after receiving his new orders, Downey would contact his new Academy supervisor.

Lieutenant Dan Precourt had been assigned to the Command and Operations School at the Academy since 1999. Downey would work for Precourt, beginning in the summer of 2000. Precourt was "born and raised in the Boston area and [despite] having cursory knowledge of the First Coast Guard District, I had never even heard of Jack Downey."[55]

Delaying the Inevitable

Precourt recalled that first phone call with the master chief explicitly. "He was calling to ask for a delay in coming to the Academy, for various operational requirements at Station Pt. Judith…an inexperienced executive petty officer, personnel turnover, lack of qualified boat coxswains etc. Certainly, all these concerns were legitimate and compelling reasons on face in the mind of an Old Salt like Master Chief Downey, especially if it could delay the dreaded shore assignment to USCGA!"[56]

Those who knew the master chief well would have known that Jack Downey, after three assignments at Point Judith, would never have a unit that wasn't squared away or didn't have enough qualified personnel, leaving a mess for the next officer in charge.

Precourt was having nothing of Downey's delay tactics and told him that if he couldn't convince the enlisted detailer to extend the master chief who was already at the Academy, then he expected the venerable legend to arrive on time. Precourt's boss at the time was Commander Mike Parks, who was nearby and sensed the tension that was obvious during the phone call. He said sarcastically, "Gee, Dan, how'd that go with the new Master Chief?"[57]

Downey arrived on time, and Precourt and Downey were not off to a great start. There was a certain irony that HQ sent the enlisted "hero of District One" to teach at the "Factory" (an affectionate euphemism for the Academy), best known for grooming new officers.

Precourt and others pressed ahead, getting the master chief up to speed on the latest classroom technology, the ship simulator and just making him comfortable in front of new audiences. Soon the fish stopped flopping around and adjusted to the new settings.

An old-school instructor might have been comfortable simply reading from the slides as a "sage on the stage," but not the Academy's latest edition. Precourt and others figured out that they just needed to let "Jack Downey be Jack Downey."[58] The Academy leadership knew that they had made a good choice when entire classes of prospective commanding officers and executive petty officers left their class howling with laughter at the endless number of Downey's sea stories and always wanted for more. They also left with tangible and valuable life lessons, or "Downey-isms."

Simple School Wisdom

One such lesson involved Downey's notional unit budget and accounting procedures. In his view it was, according to Precourt, "a matter for the leader to move a stack of Monopoly money from the bottom drawer of his desk to the waste basket with the passing of each funding requisition. No more Monopoly money, no more budget."[59]

In another classic, Downey was queried about the advisability of performing a post–search and rescue boarding of a vessel while it was still underway and being towed to shore. Downey was quick to quip, "Sure, you can change the oil on your car too while you're driving!"[60]

In time, Master Chief Downey found his stride. As an instructor, Downey fast became a campus celebrity. According to Precourt, "MCPO Jack Downey's classroom became remarkable to watch. The curriculum, instructor notes, and PowerPoint slideshows simply became props in what was the real lesson—just get Master Chief talking, the lesson would eventually find its way out. It was like listening to seafaring wisdom one could only read about in an old copy of Bowditch or Dutton's. Had I only known."[61]

Other Sides to Downey

Downey was also a closet Coast Guard historian and had a strong connection to his service's heritage and heroes. He first met his idol and mentor, Chief Warrant Officer Bernie Webber, the coxswain on the now famous *Pendleton* rescue of February 18, 1952, in 1988 when Downey took over Station Chatham. Webber took thirty-two merchant seamen off the *Pendleton* at night and during a storm that featured forty- to sixty-foot seas.

For the next five years, the master chief invited Webber back from Webber's winter home in Melbourne, Florida, each summer just to sit on the mess deck at the station to give the old salt the opportunity to listen to today's Guardsmen and occasionally pass along some ancient wisdom. "Webber would have coffee, sometimes share a meal, and reminisce about the boat. We'd also talk about the Coast Guard; the discussion would always lead to how the Coast Guard did its job."[62]

Those memories and lessons from the past stayed with the master chief, even during his time at the Academy as an instructor. Downey went so far as to single-handedly bring the famous CG36500 rescue boat to the Academy's Jacobs Rock Sailing Center piers in the late spring of 2001 in rough weather. The Orleans Historical Society, the owners of the restored vessel, had secured an additional $1,500 worth of insurance for the vessel for the one-day expedition. Downey would later lament how rough it had been on the trip from Orleans to New London in mere eight-foot seas and wondered aloud how Webber and his crew could have survived, let alone recovered thirty-two seamen from a foundering tanker. But Downey knew the value of showing the cadets the actual boat that had rescued the merchant seamen from the broken tanker in 1952.

Downey at the helm of the famous CG36500. *Brian Tague.*

Packing Plebes: A Real-Life Tactile Lesson

Downey somehow co-opted his Academy bosses' approvals to schedule time for the busy cadets in their heavily scripted two-hundred-week curriculum. He went so far as to ask thirty-six lithe cadets to attempt to wedge themselves into and onto the cramped rescue boat to simulate the night of the rescue where the four CG36500 crew members somehow shared space with the thirty-two survivors on a boat rated to carry fewer than half their numbers. The cadets could not do it, learning a valuable lesson about what survivors and Coast Guard crews can do in near-death circumstances—and they learned it in a very tactile way.

According to Downey, "Bernie's philosophy was 'we have to do better for the next generation.' To me, he seemed to be saying to always remember that someone came before you who set you up for success."[63] And Downey carried Bernie's philosophy and the story of the iconic rescue with him for the rest of his time at the Academy and well after his retirement.

One can track the master chief's post-retirement efforts to reach seven thousand cadets and other mariners in a later chapter. Or you can watch the 2016 Disney film *The Finest Hours* and see his name acknowledged at the very end of the scrolling credits. That minor accolade didn't quite appropriately acknowledge his nautical know-how and simple wisdom, even for the Hollywood elite.

There was one scene in the movie where the novice movie actor rowers were struggling to smoothly feather their oars as they used the dory to get to the venerable CG36500 rescue boat. Picture the movie's star-studded actors flailing their oars awkwardly and the boat proceeding with imprecision. Not a good look.

Frustrated by his actors' ineptness, the director asked his advisor "Jack" if he could teach the wayward crew how to row in unison. Our master chief replied, "Sure, but I've got a better idea that will save you a lot of time." More simple wisdom for the ages. And so the film crew then ably constructed a clandestine towing arrangement that would allow the stagehands to drag the dory smoothly toward its destination regardless of the actors' mistimed strokes.

The master chief's Academy supervisor would continue to teach at the Command and Operations school for a few more years, working closely with the master chief scheming, according to Precourt, to "improve the student experience, especially the cutter simulator and Rules of the Road [navigation] program. I remember fondly his laughter and the fun we had together during those long nights in the bilges of Yeaton Hall. If you couldn't get underway to train, relying only on a simulator like we did, you'd want MCPO Downey as your instructor. His decades of experience made the simulator as 'real' as one could make it."[64]

Precourt continued, "There were many days and nights together in the classroom, simulator and the local watering hole where class would continue after hours. Often accompanied by his drink of choice, Canadian Club on ice—'CC on the rocks' in his parlance—the sea stories he shared were an education unto themselves. Our relationship blossomed into a mutual respect. We had come a long way together. I learned a lot working alongside him."[65]

But the master chief proved to be a restless soul at the Academy, and although he made a huge difference in hundreds if not thousands of future Coast Guard, NOAA and international maritime leaders and operators, his mind often schemed ways to get back to the field and on the water. He worked the phones with colleagues and responded to off-campus calls for his expertise.

Any Excuse to Deploy

The Academy's 2003 endorsement to his application for the assignment year 2004 officer in charge screening panel demonstrated the breadth of his travels and influences during the three previous years at the school. In the fall of 2001, Downey was asked to serve as Coast Guard cutter *Hammerhead*'s temporary OIC for a six-week period. This was the second time he had filled in on the *Hammerhead*. The time previous occurred when the permanent OIC fell and hurt his leg in 2000.

Captain Eric Shaw, the Academy's Command and Operations school chief in 2004, indicated, "Downey was hand-picked to serve as the acting OIC of *Hammerhead* for six weeks. With no notice, he immediately assumed command and led an inexperienced crew through SEOPS training, making the cutter ready for immediate departure MHLS [Maritime Homeland Security] operations following the September 11th tragedies."[66]

Chapter 8

THE NIAGARA TRAGEDY

On March 23, 2001, four Coast Guardsmen left in a twenty-one-foot rescue boat from Station Niagara, New York, at 7:41 p.m. on a law enforcement mission in the Niagara River. Within twenty minutes, the coxswain buried the boat's bow into a Lake Ontario wave, and the boat slowly rolled to starboard and spilled the crew into chilly waters. It would be almost five hours before help arrived. Once found, two were pronounced dead at a local hospital the following morning, and two others would barely survive.

In March 2001, a former boss who led the MISHAP Analysis Board, or MAB for short, asked Downey to serve on it. MABs are required and established for all accidents with fatalities to untangle evidence and review survivor statements to learn what had happened and what caused the accident and make recommendations about how to prevent a similar accident. Downey's impact was immediately felt when other, more senior members of the board were unable to elicit a meaningful timeline from two survivors. His common-sense, "aw shucks" style of engaging the two grieving guardsmen enabled the review team to paint a vivid picture—one that changed policy and immediately garnered $2 million for scarce cold weather equipment at rescue stations. This foray as part of the Niagara MISHAP was just one instance of the master chief's escapism back to his old-world ways.

By the time of the tragedy, Downey had left Rhode Island in 2000 and was stationed at the Coast Guard Academy in New London, Connecticut. He hadn't even been at the Academy a full year when he agreed to serve on the

MAB. Captain Dana Goward, chief of search and rescue at Coast Guard Headquarters, had asked the newly formed MAB's president, another senior captain, "Who else do you want?"[67] The new leader of the MAB, Downey's former boss, quickly asked for Master Chief Downey, knowing that he was a natural communicator, especially with other boat forces' operators. The MAB president had seen Downey ably pivot between being the kindly story-telling grandfather and the harsh disciplinarian, depending on the circumstances, and knew that his skills would be needed.

Three others besides the MAB president and Downey—an engineer, a flight surgeon and retired Rear Admiral Al Steinman, USPHS, who had been the Coast Guard's chief of health and safety and had served on two previous MISHAP Analysis Boards—rounded out the team of investigators. The five-man team gathered at Station Niagara, today a part of Sector Eastern Great Lakes (then Group Buffalo), within a week of the tragedy and got to work.

Steinman knew that cold-water survival was dependent on factors like "water temperature, sea-state, physical characteristics of the survivors, protective clothing, availability of flotation and signaling devices, and behavior of the survivors in the water."[68] The Niagara crew had filed a float plan indicating that they intended to conduct an Alien Migrant Interdiction Operation (AMIO) up the nearby Niagara River. Unit experience had shown that foreign migrants had illegally attempted to float from the Canadian side of the river to the U.S. border when winter weather was moderate. Despite the thirty-six-degree air temperature, the weather was determined ideal for these illegal crossings, and a high-risk AMIO nighttime patrol was planned.

The four crewmen left the station around 7:41 p.m. and failed to respond to the first radio check at 8:01 p.m. with the Station Niagara communications watch stander. These radio checks occurred every thirty minutes on the hour and the half hour. The station watch stander was not initially alarmed because the float plan indicated that the boat was operating in "a known National Distress System (NDS) VHF-FM gray or dead zones for radio communications."[69] (The service had undertaken a full upgrade of its entire ninety-five-thousand-mile network of VHF-FM search and rescue radio systems after a horrific search and rescue case in late 1997, but system upgrades would not be made near Niagara for some time.)

Still, at 8:15 p.m., the station watch stander asked Group Buffalo's radio watch stander to use enhanced radio capabilities to reach the Station Niagara small boat crew. Group Buffalo was not aware that Station Niagara had a boat underway—a Group policy did not exist requiring it be aware of its subordinate stations' boat operations. Group Buffalo's effort to reach the four-man crew was fruitless, too.

The four-man crew also missed the 8:30 p.m. radio check. Worries escalated into further actions. Between 8:30 and 8:45 p.m., the station contacted the "acting" officer in charge and executive petty officer to report that they had lost communications with their boat. The acting OIC immediately left home and searched for his station's boat by car along the Niagara River en route to the station.

The acting OIC and the Niagara County sheriff simultaneously arrived at the station at 9:15 p.m. At 9:30 p.m., the station made notifications to Group Buffalo and the full-time OIC. The Group assumed search and rescue coordination responsibilities and began what are called "pre-communications" checks in the lower Niagara River area, the planned operational area.

By 10:20 p.m., the OIC had returned from leave to the station, and both the U.S. Coast Guard and Canadian Coast Guard launched search and rescue helicopters. Standard search efforts that focused on the boat's float plan in the Niagara River turned up nothing. Unfortunately, no one knew that they had elected to go out onto Lake Ontario before they started their official mission upriver.

The fire chief from nearby Wilson, New York, and the OIC Station Niagara later developed a plan to expand the search into Lake Ontario. The fire chief splintered off from the main search areas in the Niagara River at about 11:30 p.m. to investigate Lake Ontario. Now it was going on four and a half hours.

One survivor noticed the fire boat's approach and woke up the second survivor. Together they hailed the fire chief by waving their arms and yelling. At 12:27 a.m., the "Wilson Fire Department recovered all four crewmen within 100 yards of each other. CPR was immediately instituted on the coxswain and a crewman, and rewarming of all four boat crewmen began."[70]

Tragically, two crewmen died later that morning at a nearby hospital because of hypothermia and drowning, despite the heroic efforts of the firefighters and hospital personnel who were uniquely trained in the resuscitation of cold-water victims. The MAB's job was to find out why they had died and to make recommendations so it would not happen to any other Coast Guardsmen again. Downey's eclectic skill set would be the key in finding out the "why" and establishing a timeline that was critical to the analysis.

After a day or two, the Niagara station training room was set up for the Mishap Analysis Board's private interviews and discussions. At one point, the captain in charge of the MAB had been trying for the better part of two hours to develop a rapport with the two survivors to get information and understand exactly what happened. He was frustrated and humbled and could not make sense of the answers he was getting. He finally turned to one of the most experienced search and rescue experts in the boat forces, Master Chief Jack Downey. "I give up, maybe it's my uniform or that I'm an officer and they think they're in trouble, but I'm getting nowhere," he said to Jack. Without blinking an eye, Downey said, "Cap, I got this, go make yourself comfortable."[71] This phrase was a classic Downey-ism response to senior officers when they had waded (or stumbled) into his territory.

A Lesson About Talking to Boatswain's Mates

After a long two and half hours, the master chief emerged from the classroom with five turn charts, all marked with different coloring, with picture representations of every phase of the tragedy. A complete narrative of the accident unfolded in pictures. Miffed by his failure and somewhat envious of Jack's ability to get to the truth, the captain asked, "How did you do it?" Master Chief said, "I asked them to *draw* what happened, that's all." Jack had teased out the untenable by putting markers in the hands of the survivors. Later, he explained that "some Boatswain's mates and enlisted just do better with images (pictures) than words."[72]

Simple wisdom and inevitable truth were a hallmark of Jack's tradecraft. These representations and the narrative Downey cobbled together with images went on to become the "trunk" of the investigative tree to which each team member would add their branches and limbs of expertise.

The MAB determined that only five immersion suits were available for a station with fifteen personnel. The Niagara station was typical in its woefully inadequate inventory of cold weather immersion suits due to Coast Guard budgetary issues. Understanding that cold-water survival depends on the watertight integrity of crew immersion suits, there was no way that all five small boat crewmen had the proper "fit" to stay warm.

It was also determined that several crewmen wore cotton undergarments and incorrect headwear and that both factors contributed to the acceleration of hypothermia. Only one crewman carried the required search and rescue equipment (e.g., pyrotechnics), and this MK-79 flare device had been stepped on and was nonoperational. Furthermore, not all crew members wore law enforcement vests, as required.

Once the twenty-one-foot, nonstandard, foam-collared boat got underway, the coxswain immediately diverged from the float plan and decided to take the newest station member, a late addition to the mission, on a brief "fam" run north into Lake Ontario to see what the shoreline lights looked like at night. He did so without notifying the station of the change of plans. The result would be devastating.

The Niagara River's current was headed north into the lake directly opposite a steady onshore southerly wind, and this created steep four-to-five-foot standing or vertical waves. The air temperature was thirty-six degrees, and the visibility was clear. For about nine minutes, everything was normal as they proceeded into the lake *against* the steep four-foot waves.

About one thousand yards into the lake, the coxswain turned the boat around and began to head south toward the Niagara River and their original float plan. Now traveling *with* the waves, he used a technique called "squashing" the waves. This is when the coxswain would accelerate the boat from wave top to wave top and briefly stop on the crest of each wave. The squashing technique was appropriate for a motor lifeboat but not for their nonstandard, foam-collared boat.

Unfortunately, on one of these waves, the coxswain overshot the crest and dug the boat's bow into the backside of the next wave, causing the boat to lose steerage, slowly rolling to starboard and tossing the crew of four into the frigid lake waters. The coxswain quickly and heroically rallied his crew in the water and directed they swim away from the overturned vessel, which was bucking in the waves. He had his crew swim toward a buoy just fifty yards away. Unfortunately, none of the four would make it swimming against the river's two-knot current.

The crew struggled to keep their arms linked—a survival technique—arm over shoulder, as hypothermia began to sap their strength. No one saw the muzzle flashes from their .45-caliber handguns as they attempted to signal for help. During the next four hours, the crew gradually became separated, and two crewmen lost consciousness.

The MAB determined that the coxswain likely directed his crew to leave the overturned boat because the nonstandard boat had previously sunk at the pier (additional floatation had subsequently been added), and the overturned boat had begun to "buck" wildly in the choppy Lake Ontario waves.

The most serious determination had to do with the decision to leave the overturned twenty-one-foot rescue boat: "Had the crew of CG-213241 egressed the 36° F water and climbed atop the overturned boat, there likely would have been no deaths in this mishap. Furthermore, given where the boat was eventually found, it is possible that the crew, had they been atop the vessel, could have walked ashore near their home base."[73]

Unfortunately, the coxswain was one of the crew who didn't survive, in part because he elected to wear a so-called comfort ring in the neck of his dry suit. This was a doughnut-shaped device that stretched the rubber neck seal to allow ventilation of the suit and help prevent him from overheating under normal conditions on the boat. But once the coxswain was tossed from the boat, that same collar ring provided easy access for Lake Ontario's thirty-six-degree water, which came pouring into his suit, completely negating the protective effects of the dry suit and greatly accelerating the onset of fatal hypothermia. The MAB also determined that Coast Guard aviation rescue personnel had been issued a prohibition for using the plastic neck ring two years prior to the Niagara mishap, but the aviators and boat forces offices apparently did not share that information.

All told, the MAB made twenty-two recommendations—service-wide purchase of immersion suits for all cold weather boat forces; new D-ring designs for immersion suits so crew would be able to stay together for prolonged periods, even after prolonged exposure; enhanced operational risk procedures; new lost communications; and revised hypothermia prevention protocols, just to name a few.

Master Chief Downey received a letter of appreciation and a letter of commendation that credited him, in part, with developing "greater [service-wide] awareness of the deleterious effects of cold-water immersion, a need for greater understanding of nonstandard boat operations and an ever-increasing understanding of the need for leadership to practice operational risk management, day-to-day."[74]

Downey assimilated what he had learned during the Niagara MAB into his ongoing work at the Coast Guard Academy to memorialize lessons for future commanding officers, officers in charge and their executive petty officers. His Academy end-of-tour award reflected his ability to quickly translate new operational lessons into practical classroom learning objectives.

Most might have been satisfied with being part of an important MISHAP Analysis Board or even quickly incorporating new knowledge into the Coast Guard Academy's schoolhouse environment. But the same detail-oriented master chief who would counsel young petty officer for not properly furling a line or returning every part and piece of a Shop Vac to their proper storage place knew that there was more work to be done after the two Niagara crewmen had died. He was the proverbial "dog with a bone," and he would not let the Niagara lessons die along with the crewmen.

A few months after the Niagara MISHAP, the president of the MAB took over as the District One chief of operations in August 2001. Downey called him a few months later and said, "Hey, Cap, do you want to take a ride to Station Burlington, Vermont, and see a squared away unit that has figured out this operational risk management thing?" His former boss told him that he was a little bit busy with the post-9/11 thing but would get back to him when things simmered down.

Within a year, they were both in a Coast Guard helicopter headed from Boston to Station Burlington, Vermont, on Lake Champlain to examine how one officer in charge had figured out how to operationalize risk management at a practical level. That trip, inspired by the master chief's curiosity and determination, would lead to a 2003 formal District One operational risk management (ORM) unit-level instruction for all stations, aids to navigation teams and marine safety offices, mandating the use of "ORM to initially assess risk levels and monitor their underway missions. Used consistently, ORM will assist in planning a mission from its onset, while constantly monitoring that mission's risk weighed against its gain until mission completion. Practicing ORM will help increase our personnel's safety and reduce the likelihood of accidents by eliminating unwarranted problems caused by unnecessary risk." The master chief took the Niagara lessons and replayed the stories that kept him awake at night in his later assignment from 2002 until his 2008 retirement as the First District command master chief under Rear Admiral Tim Sullivan. The dog with a bone had the ultimate platform as District One's command master chief to convey important lessons.

At most every unit he visited, some part of the Niagara operational risk management wisdom would be imparted in meaningful ways to prevent future accidents and loss of life. Rear Admiral Steinman said it best: "Master Chief played a significant role in uncovering, investigating and subsequently addressing, resulting in service wide improvements in safety, survival, and operations for the entire small boat community. As he had done for his entire Coast Guard career, Master Chief Downey's contributions undoubtedly led to the saving of lives of Coast Guard men and women."[75]

Downey had lived through and been a pivotal part of the Coast Guard's cultural transition involving risk management in search and rescue, hearing the firsthand horror stories from his mentor and friend Bernie Webber

Rear Admiral Tim Sullivan recounts Downey's forty-two-year career during the retirement ceremonies. *Brian Tague.*

about how boat crews blindly committed to rescues that were impossible and sometimes deadly. Downey wanted to be a part of putting to rest the Coast Guard's aging unofficial adage inherited from the 1899 Regulations of the United States Life-Saving Service—"You have to go out, but you don't have to come back."[76]

Those regulations specified that a crew try all available methods, be it boat, breeches buoy or life cart, trying one and then the others in succession and not desist from their efforts until the impossibility of effecting a rescue was demonstrated.[77] This procedure sometimes put the lifesaving crews in just as much peril as the crews they went to save. This early philosophy had become part of the USLSS's early culture and had persisted for several decades after the 1915 establishment of the U.S. Coast Guard.

Downey knew that modern risk management guidelines and updated regulations, some of which he had recommended modifications to or helped create, were designed to keep crews safer when doing their jobs. Part of his legacy was to ensure that all future boat crews understood and could measure the risks associated with attempting a rescue with the value of the crews' lives.

Chapter 9

COMMANDING CUTTER *HAMMERHEAD* ONE LAST TIME

In July 2004, Downey stepped aboard *Hammerhead* as the officer in charge for the third time, this time as *the* officer in charge, not a fill-in. The eighty-seven-foot patrol boat was moored in Little Harbor, Massachusetts, right next to its parent command, Coast Guard Group Woods Hole. All things considered, his tour at the Coast Guard Academy had been successful. The master chief, as usual, credited his success more to the people he worked with and not the bureaucracy of academia that often permeated academic institutions. There was no mistaking it—getting underway was much preferred to sitting behind a desk.

Downey's first tour aboard *Hammerhead* was when he was OIC at station Point Judith and temporarily and concurrently took command of the Marine Protector–class coastal patrol boat while the skipper recovered from a leg fracture. That tour included responding to EgyptAir 990 crashing offshore, sixty miles south of Nantucket, on October 31, 1999. *Hammerhead* spent eight difficult days retrieving personal memorabilia that was strewn across miles of open ocean. Crew members were debriefed and defused after this critical incident, with many recalling the disruptive images of children's clothes, shoes and toys being among their most vivid memories and nightmares.

His second tour in *Hammerhead* would follow soon thereafter and was just as challenging. Downey was pulled from the Coast Guard Academy's staff to augment the *Hammerhead*'s twenty-four-hour watches, pacing the waters of New York Harbor immediately after September 11, 2001. In addition to *Hammerhead*'s general responsibility to patrol and secure New York Harbor, there was the heightened obligation to specifically protect "America's symbol of freedom"—the Statue of Liberty—and other important landmarks, including the United Nations Building overlooking the East River and the Verrazzano Bridge at the mouth of New York Harbor. Throughout the post-9/11 tour, *Hammerhead* mingled among the many tugs that were shepherding commercial freighters and tankers into the harbor, disappearing into city's skyline shrouded in a blanket of bright lights.

Hammerhead's new tasking after Downey took over a third time was simpler and more routine. His orders were to patrol New England with port and waterway security details, including fishery patrols, coastal search and rescue duty, the occasional environmental protection response and the ever-present possibility of submarine escort duty in eastern Long Island Sound.

For two years, Downey and the crew of *Hammerhead* answered the call. They responded to many demanding operations throughout the Coast Guard's First District, covering the area from the Maine-Canadian border to the northern tip of New Jersey.

Downey's crew conducted more than seventy law enforcement boardings, many within difficult and high-threat areas. These included commercial fishing boardings resulting in violations, fines and vessel permit sanctions for fishing in areas that were closed to commercial fishing. They conducted multiple rescue and assistance operations, including coming to the aid of a commercial fishing vessel that was taking on water seventeen miles south of Nantucket. Within minutes of arriving on scene, using dewatering pumps, the *Hammerhead* crew saved the vessel and its three crew members.[78]

During the United Nations General Assembly's World Summit in 2005, *Hammerhead* led the security zone enforcement effort for surrounding water areas and other units, including the Coast Guard's New York–based Maritime Safety and Security Team (a team of highly trained law enforcement personnel) and other regional agencies. Collectively, the waterborne security effort oversaw 164 boardings (including 22 high-interest commercial vessels) and 35 marine distress cases and spent many hours performing positive control measures to prevent potential threats.[79]

In addition to his duties as OIC on *Hammerhead*, Downey was also singled out to oversee the Ready-for-Sea certification for the newest eighty-seven-footer, the cutter *Tiger Shark*. And as the Coast Guard's first Ancient Keeper, he made time to speak with passion, humor and wisdom throughout New England, inspiring civilian and Coast Guard audiences about the historic rescue by the crew of the CG36500 and of the Coast Guard's traditions of "Honor, Respect and Devotion to Duty."

Commandant Tom Collins presents Downey with the First Ancient Keeper Award with Lory Newmeyer, director of the Hull Lifesaving Museum, November 2003. *Brian Tague.*

Despite a tight schedule, when asked to participate in a chief's initiation and a twenty-four-hour "Stand-at-Attention" fundraiser, Downey readily agreed. He provided the audience of prospective chief petty officers with insights into his four decades of service. Downey began his dialogue with a preamble about his "words of wisdom" for the new crop of leaders. He reminded them to "always look aft before moving ahead, and to look for people in their wake. To recognize their wake as a safe and productive course to follow and not just a sign of one's departure while trying to survive the turbulence."[80]

Downey continued and reminded the assembled prospective chiefs that "the PRESENT becomes the PAST and that the PRESENT and the PAST are gifts to the FUTURE. To always remember that their performance and how they work for and with people, coupled with their good DEEDS in the PRESENT, becomes the PAST and their gift and legacy to the FUTURE. As CHIEFS they are now the PRESENT, PAST and FUTURE of the Coast Guard," closing with, "CARRY ON, keep up the outstanding performance—project those good deeds and take care of our Coast Guard. It is all about the Core Values of the Coast Guard—HONOR, RESPECT & DEVOTION TO DUTY."[81]

At a time in his career when some might extol their own virtues and storied careers, Downey reminded his audience of future chief petty officers to look over their shoulders and make sure the people that they led, or were going to lead, were sailing smoothly and safely. This was a hallmark of Downey's life ethos, be it in or out of uniform, on duty, with his family or retired.

Over Memorial Day weekend in 2005, Downey again carved out time to support an event on Cape Cod, Troops in the Spotlight. It required volunteer participants to stand at attention for twenty-four hours, either individually or in a relay team. The event organizer, Lieutenant Colonel K.J. Stillings, USMC, praised the master chief for his participation, commenting that Downey's "dedication to duty and unselfishness set an example for not only his peers to follow, but every American as well. Through Downey's efforts over $6,000 and seven truckloads of donations were raised to mail care package to Marines, soldiers, sailors, and airmen stationed abroad." He further praised Downey for his tireless efforts during the holiday weekend and for a job well done.[82]

Downey's reputation to both volunteer for and orchestrate charitable events was well known, but he was also better known and respected as a no-nonsense chief with witty solutions. Chief Steve Babcock remembered the chief at the Group. "I met and worked with Master Chief while assigned as Supply Department SKC at Group Woods Hole/Sector SE New England, 2005–2009. He served as OIC at several of the units. He was always outspoken on the Mess, offering no-nonsense solutions. I remember him wearing his Combo cover with his work uniform. As the Sector Contracting Officer and Properly Officer, Master Chief and I didn't always agree but he was always fair."[83]

Chief Warrant Officer Christine Bouressa, who served on *Hammerhead*, also remembered the chief, in addition to one of his witty solutions. "The sector YN was giving him the run around for administrative tasks he needed help with. The YN kept pushing the motto: 'Member's Responsibility.' So, Master Chief grabbed a piece of line, stomped across the parking lot, and plopped the line on the YN's desk. The YN was confused. MC told him to tie him a bowline. The YN said he didn't know how to; it wasn't his job. So, MC replied, 'Good, so how about you do YOUR job, and I'll do MY job then?' The YN took care of MC's admin issue after that."[84]

When Downey departed *Hammerhead* in August 2006, he received his fourth commendation medal. The cutter *Hammerhead* was his last command and his last afloat tour. He was nearly sixty years old and had accrued forty years of service. He wondered what would come next. Had retirement crossed his mind, even if it was only that veil of dull light that sneaks over the horizon before the sun rises? But he didn't look back, only ahead. There was no reason to look back.

After pondering his career, thoughts of his family had to have come next, especially those of his wife, Judith. Downey had known that she had held their family together over the years when he was "somewhere on duty." Additionally, relatives had died, and his children had grown, married and had children of their own. One of his simple pleasures was playing on the living room floor with his grandchildren when he did make it home, and he wanted more of it.

But Downey's no-nonsense approach and witty solutions had traveled farther than the Group and the patrol boat. They had spread like folklore throughout the First District and beyond. People had noticed, and the outcome landed him another billet. Not everyone thought the billet and the outspoken chief were a good match, not even the venerable service's first Ancient Keeper. Some just scratched their heads, while others said, "No way." Out of the blue, Downey had been considered for the First District's command master chief billet. Would he fend off retirement one more time?

Chapter 10

A NEW TYPE OF DISTRICT ONE COMMAND MASTER CHIEF

Downey's thoughts about retiring took a back seat when he was offered another billet in the First District. Admiral Timothy Sullivan was reporting as the new district commander, and Downey was favorably considered to be the First District's command master chief (CMC). The First District's area of responsibility spanned from the Canadian border south to Toms River, New Jersey, and included parts of New York waters. District CMCs are the district commander's right hand and principal advisor on all matters operational and personnel. Behind the Coast Guard's master chief petty officer of the Coast Guard in Washington, the ten district CMCs were viewed as the most influential enlisted personnel in a service with thirty-nine thousand active-duty members, civilians and reserves.

As Admiral Sullivan recalled, "I had not sailed in the New England area since 1998 but when I saw his name on the short list of potential Command Master Chiefs, I didn't hesitate for a second to pick up the phone and asked him to take the position. To say the least, his name and reputation preceded him well. In fact, his name had become almost lore in New England, and many have even gone so far as to use the term *legend*."[85]

While Sullivan was aware of Downey's "lead from the front" reputation, he had never met him. But he believed that the "true blue sailor" was the right man for the job, which required keen listening skills and discretion to resolve issues among Coast Guard members and their families. Sullivan had heard stories loosely based on hearsay. One Downey gem was when he worked at the Coast Guard Academy. During a testy conference in a "breaking all the rules" pitch to change the Coast Guard's culture, Downey said, "You've been working on this for your entire career(s) and have spent $500K, why now?"[86] Sullivan didn't see this type of comment as an issue, rather a needed probe at getting to the truth.

Solving issues and working initiatives were nothing new for Downey, but this effort stretched across not merely one unit that he was personally responsible for—it would stretch across all units covering two thousand miles of coastline, impacting 2,600 active-duty, reserve and auxiliary personnel throughout eight Northeast states that others were managing. Considering these unchartered waters, to help quell Downey's angst, he called on his trusted friend Master Chief Petty Officer Skip Bowen. Skip Bowen recalled, "I knew MCPO Jack Downey from the time when he was part of an administrative investigation when I was OIC of CGC *Hammerhead*....I also knew him from my time as Admiral Thad Allen's E10 [CMC of the Coast Guard] and he was Admiral Sullivan's CMC at D1. I remember him calling me for advice about becoming the D1 CMC and I told him, 'You're going to have to start answering your phone and checking your e-mails.'"[87]

Downey had logistical concerns, one of which was distance. He lived eighty miles from the Coast Guard District office building in Boston and knew firsthand the horror stories of Boston traffic. Downey thought that the best thing to do was what he'd always done: address his concerns straight on. Downey reported to the District Building and sat with Admiral Sullivan in his corner office overlooking Boston Harbor. From the upper floor of the eight-story building, there was a clear view of Logan Airport across the harbor, President's Road, the Main Ship Channel, the Charlestown Monument and the Tobin Bridge.

Built in 1918, the John Foster Williams Building, named for a captain in the Revenue Cutter Service, served as a support building to the nearby customs house, located several blocks inland. The Williams Building served as a warehouse for storage, inspections and seizure of goods operations. Today, the building houses offices for the Coast Guard's New England command and several other federal agencies.

Downey tried to torpedo his own chances of getting the job by admitting that he was far from being the Coast Guard's poster boy. He was a tad overweight, still liked to have a smoke and an occasional elixir of Canadian Club on the rocks and was not tech-savvy with e-mails and text messaging. Sullivan was not dissuaded and reviewed Downey's operational, command and staff assignments covering forty years of service and his many awards. Admiral Sullivan was satisfied that Downey wouldn't be a "yes man" and would deliver the truth—good, bad or indifferent. He'd also fix the unfixable that most others would cringe at and avoid as being too risky for their careers.

Downey tried one last pitch and addressed his commuting concern. After a brief discussion, the response is simple. The admiral wanted to visit every unit, and Downey needed to be with him. An itinerary would be forthcoming, otherwise he wanted Downey in the field with the operational forces and not in the office. Travel at will and stay in touch. Downey retooled and sailed his second big brown desk from August 2006 until his retirement in June 2008. He shed some pounds, stopped smoking "cold turkey" (no patches or programs) and learned how to e-mail and text. He surpassed all expectations and addressed concerns with diplomacy throughout the chain of command.

Fellow BMCM and Command Master Chief William James remembered Downey's ability to get the message across and succeed in the most unexpected places: "Jack was the First District Command Master Chief (CMC) when I was the Atlantic Area CMC, 2006–2008. Like me, this was Jack's first full-time CMC assignment for a Flag Officer, so we both were newcomers in a community where others had homesteaded for a while. At our first Flag Officer and CMC meeting, I got together with the LANT District CMCs and laid out my expectations: the CMCs didn't work for me, but their bosses worked for MY boss, so we needed to freely share all information that the Flag Officers may discuss, so we can be prepared to give our best advice."[88]

James had been a master chief for seven years at the time and became a CMC after three consecutive tours as officer in charge afloat. He had a great working relationship with his flag officer, VADM Brian Peterman. Even James admitted that he had trepidation leading that bunch of CMCs, especially Jack, considering Downey advanced to chief when he was in grade school. James observed, "Time and again, Jack showed that he 'got it,' our relationship, much better than the other District CMCs. Jack always called to let me know of noteworthy issues in his District One units, and in my LANT units homeported in D1. I had issues with some of the 'younger' CMCs, and always told them to call Jack to hear how our relationship was supposed to work—[for] those that did, our relationship greatly improved, to the betterment of the Coast Guardsmen we served."

James was also able to do a favor for Jack one time. Downey phoned James after calls came in from the family of an army soldier deployed to Iraq. That soldier hadn't been in touch with family, which was unusual. The New England family knew the Coast Guard better than the U.S. Army, and Jack Downey was the CG legend in the area. Luckily, James had attended a Command Senior Enlisted Leader course with DoD E-9s and called his

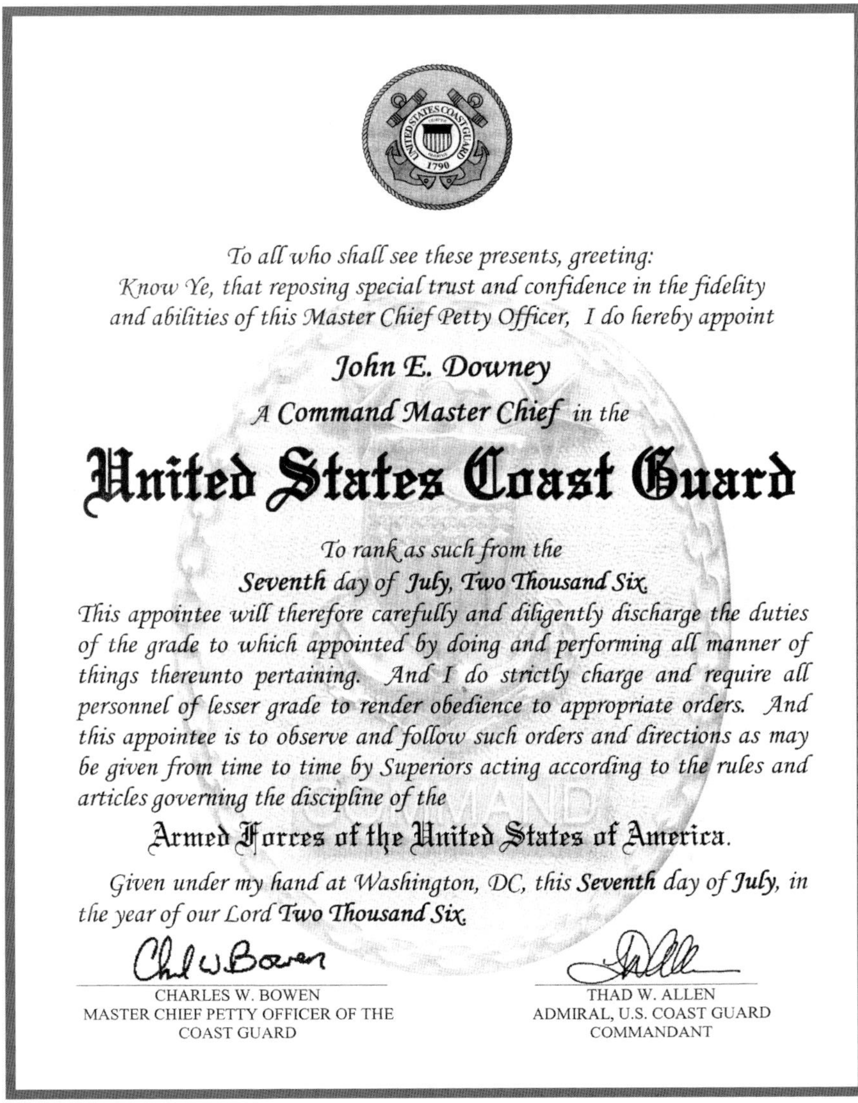

To all who shall see these presents, greeting:
Know Ye, that reposing special trust and confidence in the fidelity and abilities of this Master Chief Petty Officer, I do hereby appoint

John E. Downey
A Command Master Chief *in the*

United States Coast Guard

To rank as such from the
Seventh** day of **July, Two Thousand Six.
This appointee will therefore carefully and diligently discharge the duties of the grade to which appointed by doing and performing all manner of things thereunto pertaining. And I do strictly charge and require all personnel of lesser grade to render obedience to appropriate orders. And this appointee is to observe and follow such orders and directions as may be given from time to time by Superiors acting according to the rules and articles governing the discipline of the

Armed Forces of the United States of America.

*Given under my hand at Washington, DC, this **Seventh** day of **July**, in the year of our Lord **Two Thousand Six.***

CHARLES W. BOWEN
MASTER CHIEF PETTY OFFICER OF THE COAST GUARD

THAD W. ALLEN
ADMIRAL, U.S. COAST GUARD
COMMANDANT

Master Chief Downey's July 2006 "Command Master Chief" certificate for District One. *Brian Tague.*

classmate with Army Forces Command. James passed on the ID information he'd received from Jack—name, grade, unit and hometown—and hung up, hoping for the best but not expecting Big Army to track down one junior soldier in a war zone. Later that day, a happy Jack called to say the soldier had contacted her family and that all was well. "I was glad to have played a role in helping burnish Jack's reputation as THE man to call with any problem. I also enjoyed picturing the string of calls from ARFORCOM Command Sgt. Major to the Division CSM, down through Battalion to the Company First Sergeant—then that burly soldier grabbing that young Specialist by the collar and saying, 'Call your mom!' Oh, if that Company 1SG only knew ol' Salty Jack of the Coast Guard had initiated that tasker for him!"[89]

In his final days in Boston, Downey was awarded the Legion of Merit, having distinguished himself through superior professional expertise, leadership and dedication. He had resolved personnel and operational issues, championed a service-wide revision, updated assignment priorities and continued speaking engagements from Recruit Basic Training to Chief's Academy and Boat Forces Command School. Downey had more accumulative time as an OIC than any other member and is considered the utmost expert and primary reference in all boat force matters.[90]

For decades, Master Chief Downey had become the go-to ancient mariner about what to do and what not to do when rescuing someone who was at peril at sea. There were manuals and blue books, cheat sheets and how-to guides, but the spoken word of Downey had raised crews' awareness and had supplied them with knowledge and confidence for decades. When Downey departed Boston as the First District's command master chief in June 2008, many were sad to see him go. But many suspected that the next billet that Downey would fill would be in Kingston, Rhode Island: retirement. "It's time to go," Jack said.

Chapter 11

RETIREMENT

Jack retired on June 20, 2008, in a formal ceremony at Station Point Judith. The party went on for hours. Jack dressed in uniform one last time, with medals and a "fruit salad" of ribbons adorning his left chest. When Jack, Judith and his family arrived, crews were draping tables in white cloths, with chafing dishes on top, coffee pots and boxes of lunch supplies.

The Downeys saw an open twenty-six-foot Monomoy surfboat, a forty-four-foot motor lifeboat, a forty-seven-foot motor lifeboat and an eighty-seven-foot patrol boat—the CGC *Hammerhead*—anchored in a straight line paralleling the coastline about two hundred yards offshore. Hundreds attended the ceremony, which began at 11:00 a.m. when a bugler played Assembly, alerting guests to sit. Master of ceremony—and Downey's old friend and protégé—Chief Warrant Officer Tom Guthlein introduced the official party, followed by the presentation of the colors and an invocation.

The Coast Guard's vice-commandant, Vice-Admiral Vivien Crea, delivered remarks, touching on the history of the Coast Guard, beginning with the Revenue Cutter and Life-Saving Services and, of course, Joshua James. She closed with the thought that despite modern technologies, such as radar and the global positioning satellite system, in the end, it's people who save lives.

Jack spoke next, his remarks peppered with emotion and humor. He thanked his family for their support. He was honored and proud to have served and been trusted with the many taskings he'd received over the years and colleagues who have helped him meet those many challenges. He

Master Chief and Judith Downey depart his retirement ceremony with honors, June 2008. *Brian Tague.*

was amazed at the gains of technology and the changes in the service. He believed that mission and vision guided by deck plate leadership were key. Leadership included having a sense of accountability and self-evaluation that transcended all other requirements and for one to never be satisfied with the status quo.

Jack then surrendered the Ancient Keeper's hat to the service's second Ancient Keeper, CWO Kevin Galvin, in a short relief ceremony.

Senior Chief Gordon McClay, another friend and protégé, then took the podium and kicked off phase two of the event: Downey's official retirement ceremony. Rear Admiral Sullivan, Commander First Coast Guard District and Downey's immediate supervisor, continued the ceremony. In his remarks, he focused on Downey's longevity—Downey had served in the Coast Guard before a man even landed on the moon—professionalism and forward-thinking, highlighted by his advocacy for new rescue capabilities to dovetail with the safety of the crews and the inaugural use of risk management for New England boat crews.

Admiral Sullivan passed the podium to Senior Chief Sheila Lucey, another Downey friend and acolyte. Lucey called on two of Downey's grandchildren, Jayson and Justyn Sanford. As the Coast Guard Band began

Downey in full form at his retirement. *Brian Tague.*

Rear Admiral Sullivan; CWO Kevin J. Galvin, the Prospective Ancient Keeper (no. 2); and Master Chief Downey at his retirement ceremony. *Brian Tague.*

Bottom: Downey's grandsons Jayson and Justyn present their grandfather's ceremonial flag to an honor guard member at the retirement ceremony. *Brian Tague.*

CWO Guthlein salutes Master Chief Downey after conveying him the ceremonial retirement flag. *Brian Tague.*

to play again, a host of service members from seamen to chief warrant officers assembled on stage. Downey's grandsons participated in the flag passing ceremony to honor the family's service and their grandfather. Jayson started by passing the flag that would end nearly a dozen people later with Master Chief Downey, or simply "Pop" to Jayson and Justyn.

After the flag passing ceremony, Downey took to the podium for his second set of remarks. He again thanked his family for all their support and partially paraphrased from a training school letter dating back to the World War II era, stating that "hard jobs are routine in our service. The Coast Guard is no place for a quitter, a crybaby or a four-flusher or anyone who can't keep their eye on the ball." He reminded the crews to focus on technical expertise, professional character, loyalty, communication and heritage, urging everyone to think about how a stronger future means preparing for tomorrow today. After the benediction and retirement of colors, it was time for lunch.

Downey would not sit idle for long and transitioned from active duty to his retirement job as the Narraganset harbormaster. But he always had a strong connection to the Coast Guard's history, especially the 1952 *Pendleton* rescue off Chatham. He had been invited by his former boss and a Cape Cod historian and author to retell the story of the famous 1952 *Pendleton* rescue to thousands of cadets and mariners over the next eight years.

Chapter 12

TIMELESS LESSONS IN LEADERSHIP

The Master Chief's Last Words About His Mentor

Six months before he died, Downey delivered his final Coast Guard–related remarks on February 18, 2022. The event marked the seventieth anniversary of the *Pendleton* rescue and was hosted at the Chatham Bars Inn, providing a vista of the same ocean area where thirty-two seamen from the broken T-2 oil tanker were rescued by the four-man Coast Guard crew aboard the CG36500 motor lifeboat. The venue overlooked the famous Fish Pier and the same treacherous Chatham sandbar that Bernie Webber and his ramshackle crew had crossed seven decades ago. But on this day, unlike seventy years before, a cold chill was present, but the placid water resembled a flat, calm lake.

The day was tiring for Jack. Downey had taken part in several of the day's events, which began earlier with the Station Chatham crew laying a wreath at the site of the *Pendleton*'s sinking just offshore. Near sunset, Downey was with Admiral Tom Allen, First Coast Guard District commander, kibitzing as he normally would have, animated with hand gestures and cracking jokes.

A Coast Guard Jayhawk helicopter slowly escorted Station Chatham's new forty-five-foot Rigid Hull boat into the harbor. The sleek new craft itself was a sign of the times—there would soon be no heavy weather boats at Station

Left: Master Chief Downey holding court at the Fish Pier, Chatham, on the seventieth anniversary of the *Pendleton* rescue, 2022. *Authors' collection.*

Right: Downey wears a jacket that chronicles the fishing boats rescued during his time at Station Chatham. *Authors' collection.*

Chatham, another transition toward "efficiency." The chopper paused in a low hover for ninety seconds in full view of the hundreds of respectful gatherers on the Fish Pier. The minute and a half marked two seconds of silence for each of the forty-one *Pendleton* crew and the four rescuers, all claimed by time, some during the rescue.

The event moved to the Chatham Bars Inn for appetizers, libations and more speeches and acknowledgements for the rescuers and those who had found and preserved the historic CG36500 rescue boat. It had been a long day already by the time Jack gave his talk, and he was visibly tired.

The master chief was accompanied during the evening event by his wife of fifty-four years, Judith, and daughter Jennifer. There was a marked visible decline to Jack—he was unusually unsure of himself, unlike past public appearances. For the first time, he spoke from cue cards instead of his routine of extemporaneous and colorful dialogue. But what he said was nevertheless meaningful, timeless and respectful of his mentor and the Coast Guard he loved.

The Letter

Jack, visibly emotional and close to tears, read haltingly from a 2006 letter from Bernie Webber when Webber had heard that Downey was previously taking the District One command master chief job: "Good news! You'll be around on active duty for a while longer. I won't be able to attend, but I wanted to send you something of a personal nature. First, a replica of Chatham Station is to remind you of your days in charge at that station and those you met along the way. It's so big, you can put it on your desk, or in a drawer, of course."[91]

It was clear from the letter that each man, a legend in his own different right, had a mutual respect that transcended time and space. Webber went on to say in his letter, "I've been saving a copy [Jack narrated, "I was hesitant to read this, but I think it's…"] I have saved copy of book number 3 for the *Chatham: The Life Boat Men*, a limited edition of 300. I've been saving it all those years since the publication [1985] for a very special person. Copies number 1 and number 2 went to [Webber's wife] Miriam and my daughter Patricia. Jack, you are ***that*** person, and I hope you understand how much I appreciate the service that you've done for the CG36500." And Bernie

Senior Chief Lucey (*background*) and Downey share a moment on the famous CG36500 rescue boat after his daughter Rebecca was married at Station Brant Point, 2004. *Brian Tague.*

added as he ended the letter, "I grow too old. Hope our paths will cross once, again, and we can talk over a cup of joe. Wishing you all the best in your new assignment."[92]

The Origins of the Legends' Relationship

Webber passed suddenly in the arms of his wife, Miriam, at his Melbourne, Florida home a little more than three years after he wrote this final letter, his last, to Downey. Downey had been stationed at Chatham from 1988 to 1993 when their relationship first began and when Jack played a pivotal role by helping the Orleans Historical Society (OHS) with its work to rehabilitate the venerable CG36500. OHS volunteer Bill Quinn and his son, Bill Jr., had found the derelict CG36500 behind the National Seashore Superintendent's Office in September 1981.

Father and son had gone to an auction at the National Seashore Marconi site. Bill Jr. recalled his dad saying, "There's an old 'double ender' [thirty-six-footer] over there I want to look at. As we got closer, he said 'I know those numbers.' This started what felt like a two-month endeavor to find out what the Seashore intended to do with the boat. Seashore officials explained the intent was restoration, but lack of funding made this impossible. Dad asked if they might let it go to some organization that would restore it to a floating museum, and they agreed. By November 1991, the Orleans Historical Society (OHS) had essentially taken ownership of the restoration. Dad's army of volunteers was formed. I never went to the building when there wasn't at least 20 people inside painting, scraping paint, cleaning."[93]

Downey's involvement in the CG36500 restorations began seven years later in 1988 while assigned to Station Chatham. Then he offered to have some of his Coast Guard crew assist OHS with the boat's basic repairs and maintenance. On many occasions, the CG36500 would be hauled out at the Chatham station and worked on by OHS volunteers and Downey's crew. Downey viewed this as an opportunity for his crews to learn service history in a tangible way and integrate into the local community.

The CG36500 to the Rescue, Again!

Downey later went from Chatham to Nantucket in 1993, and so did the CG36500. One of OHS's key volunteers, Richard Ryder Jr., recalled, "Dad

Judith and Jack Downey pose with their youngest daughter, Rebecca, in 2004 on her wedding day, with Brant Point Light in the background. Notice the decorative wedding wreath instead of the customary Christmas wreath. *Brian Tague.*

told me once that the CG36500 was in Nantucket and the Coasties were doing some minor painting. The Chief [Downey] had called Dad because of two of their [Coast Guard] 44 footers were out of service, they wanted to use the CG36500 for some harbor responses. Imagine being on a boat being rescued by the famed CG36500. And this was years before the movie."[94]

Jack's remarks during the seventieth *Pendleton* anniversary celebration paid a final homage to Webber, the man he had respected since his first days in the Coast Guard in 1966. Ironically, 1966 was the year that Bernie retired from the service and Jack joined the Coast Guard. While Downey and Webber's relationship had begun in 1988, the seventieth celebration was not the first formal occasion where Jack played a pivotal role in honoring his idol. In 2002, the Coast Guard would attempt to treat the four rescuers and their families differently and more favorably than the service had immediately after the 1952 rescue, when their heroism made global headlines. Downey played a key role in softening Webber's reception to the "new" Coast Guard of 2002, which had become more appreciative of its history and heroes.

The 2002 Reunion

On a chilly, cloudy evening on May 1, 2002, Jack Downey met up with Bernie Webber and the three other Gold Medal lifesaving crew members in the lobby of Mariners House in Boston's North End. Mariners House was the site of the start of a fiftieth reunion for Webber's crew. A dinner in Boston that evening kicked off a series of events. The gathering stirred up memories of the rescue.

In the weeks after the 1952 rescue, "hero" status wasn't what it was cracked up to be for Webber. He loathed attention. The Coast Guard paraded Bernie around at events like a living recruitment poster. For years, Webber was miffed that only he and not his entire crew were guests of honor at a series of dinners to tout the rescue. To Bernie's credit, at his insistence, Richard Livesey, Ervin Maske and Andy Fitzgerald received the rare Gold Lifesaving Medal when senior Coast Guard officials had offered his crew only the lesser Silver Lifesaving Medal. By contrast, an officer received the Gold Lifesaving Medal, and his crew the Silver, when they rescued surviving seamen from the *Fort Mercer*, the *Pendleton*'s sister ship, which also split in two on the same night.

A New Coast Guard?

With Webber still leery of senior leaders decades later, in late 2001, it took months of negotiations to convince him to attend the fiftieth anniversary celebration. The initial offer was for just the crew, not the families, to be included in the fiftieth ceremonies. In the end, Webber got his way in 2002, just like he had with his crew's Gold Medals in 1952, and the families were given invitational travel orders with all expenses paid.

Downey was a haven for Bernie and his family during that emotional three-day 2002 reunion. Jack's more-than-friendship with Bernie Webber went way back. Years before, Jack had invited Bernie to visit Station Chatham, beginning when Downey first took control of Station Chatham in 1988, whenever Bernie visited his old stomping grounds on Cape Cod, where the Webbers owned a vacation home in Eastham. They struck up a genuine friendship as kindred spirits.

On the occasions of Webber's visits to Station Chatham, he'd sit on the mess deck and hold court, listening to lifesavers and, when prompted, reminisce, all under the watchful eye of the officer in charge. Was it adoration or respect or a combination of both? Either way, it was clear that Jack revered the icon of the greatest small boat rescue in Coast Guard history.

Downey's respect for Webber and service history went beyond coffee and leadership chats on the mess deck. He would play a pivotal role in 2002 when the Coast Guard honored Webber and his CG36500 on the fiftieth anniversary of the *Pendleton* rescue.

Downey was at that dinner in May 2002 when Bernie and the other Gold Medal Lifesavers met in the hotel lobby before walking to dinner just outside in Boston's North End. Jack stood in the foyer of Mariners House in 2002 when all four Gold Medal crewmen met for the first time in fifty years. This time, their wives stood beside them, along with some of the Gold Medal crew's adult children and grandchildren.

Also present was Charlie Bridges, a soft-spoken Floridian and *Pendleton* crewmen. Charlie was eighteen in 1952 and woke up to a ship torn in half. He rushed from one compartment to another, raising the alarm to his own crewmen. The event's coordination team had scoured the internet to find surviving *Pendleton* crewmen, and Charlie was one of the few remaining who could make the 2002 reunion. Charlie's wife had accompanied him. Bernie broke the ice.

The next morning in 2002 kicked off events, including a Heroes' Luncheon at the Coast Guard base on Commercial Street in Boston with guests including Congressman Bill Delahunt and Coast Guard admirals, followed by another dinner near the North End. The reunion moved to Cape Cod, where a well-attended ceremony at Coast Guard Station Chatham—known in 1952 as the Chatham Motor Lifeboat Station—was conducted. Jack even piloted Bernie and his Gold Medal crew around the harbor for old times' sake.

The afternoon slipped into evening and ended with a celebratory dinner at the Chatham Wayside Inn, a well-known restaurant nearby just off Main Street. Everyone said their farewells and departed the following morning. The Coast Guard provided several vehicles to transport the CG36500 crew and their families to airports.

Jack was there throughout, offering a friendly word to all, helping where he could and being an all-around gentleman. Jack had always

Downey at helm of CG36500, with Chief Warrant Officer Bernie Webber, during the *Pendleton*'s fiftieth anniversary at Station Chatham, 2002. *U.S. Coast Guard District One, Defense Information Distribution Service.*

reverently stood on Bernie's shoulders and provided a model just as Jack had done for emerging generations of enlisted personnel during his forty-two service years.

Several days after the formal reunion had ended, Bernie and his wife, Miriam, returned to Florida. The reunion was a meaningful event for Bernie and his crew, too. The fellowship that Jack Downey extended to Bernie and his crew was a huge part of the reunion's success. Bernie seemed to enjoy the reunion now that his crew had been treated well. Jack helped Bernie put the reunion into perspective—the Coast Guard was what it was in circa 1952, but now the service appreciated its enlisted heroes as humans and not just as public relations tools.

Timeless Lessons in Leadership

The years spilled by. The principal reunion coordinators and Jack kept in touch via e-mail and the occasional phone call. Several years after the 2002 reunion, the taped interviews that had been conducted at Mariners House with Bernie and other lifesavers Andy Fitzgerald, Ervin Maske and Richard

Livesey formed the basis for a book on the rescue. The 2007 first edition ended up on the Commandant's Recommended Reading List for Leadership and morphed into a lecture series complemented by a PowerPoint, called Timeless Lessons in Leadership. Jack was quickly included in the program after his retirement.

Between 2008 and 2016, the Timeless Lessons in Leadership program was presented before listening audiences at the Coast Guard Academy, the Massachusetts Maritime Academy, SUNY Maritime, the U.S. Merchant Marine Academy, Norwich University and at a few other places, including one-off lectures at the Maine Maritime Academy in Castine and the Wardroom Club at Coast Guard District One in Boston. In total, the *Pendleton* rescue story was recounted to more than seven thousand mariners.

Jack contributed the color commentary. He used a sense of scale, like how tall the waves were or how small the door to the survival compartment was where *Pendleton* crewmen sought shelter. "About the size of this podium's width, no more than three feet," he'd say. Or, "Picture waves twice the height of this auditorium ceiling," painting a realistic picture of the rescue circumstances. He was truly gifted and often rewarded with a line of cadet and mariner questions after the formal lectures. Sometimes, those who asked questions would follow him for a bite to eat and more conversation afterward. The lines of students that formed after each talk to speak to Jack once the lectures were over were truly memorable.

In between the years of the leadership series, as these things go, the dreaded phone calls came. First to pass was Richard Livesey in 2007. Then Bernie died suddenly in 2009. Ervin Maske was behind the wheel of an empty school bus and suffered a heart attack in 2013. Charlie Bridges, the last known *Pendleton* survivor, also died in 2013. The Timeless Lessons in Leadership team helped Casey Sherman and Michael Tougias with their best-selling book. Andy Fitzgerald hung on—even contributing recollections to producers of Disney's 2016 major motion picture *The Finest Hours*, which depicted a dramatized account of the 1952 rescue. Still, it was a good movie! And Andy passed away in November 2018 at the age of eighty-seven. All the while, the Timeless team and Jack continued with the Leadership Series.

Downey performed flawlessly during lectures. Those who heard him could never forget his raspy voice and animated ways when he recounted a yarn, a tale, a story about his days in the Coast Guard to an enraptured audience. His two co-presenters were just the crew who got to set the stage for his color commentary. Jack never really turned off the charm, nor did he miss an opportunity to provide mentorship.

The presenters often dined following a lecture, as their schedules and family lives permitted, to decompress and dissect what went right and how the Series could be improved. One time, dinner took place at this wonderful Italian place, Mezza Luna, in Buzzards Bay along the Cape Cod Canal. Mezza Luna was minutes from the Massachusetts Maritime Academy, where the lecture had just been presented to an auditorium full of cadets. Jack accepted an invitation to eat at Mezza Luna along with the son of one of the co-presenters and his two friends. The three young men got to fully experience the moment and pick up a few hints about life. But the real lesson came at dinner over plates of chicken parmesan.

Jack was asked to "tell the boys what the real secret of life is," his co-presenter remembered, not really thinking that the question would amount to anything. The boys' gazes pivoted to Jack, who put down his fork, smiled and thought for a second. "It's really simple, guys," he said. "You do the right thing the right way, for the right reason, at the right time." Though simply put in a way that young men in college could absorb and understand instantly, Jack had sophisticatedly reduced to one sentence what, as a parent, had taken years to articulate.

Paying It Forward

Eighteen months after Jack's death, the concept of the Timeless Lessons in Leadership from the *Pendleton* rescue was revived by a group of officers from the Coast Guard Academy class of 1976, and in June and July 2024, they administered a program that was given to every member, close to three hundred of the third-year class that would train the new class of plebes. The academy program interpreted the actions of Warrant Officer Webber and the *Pendleton*'s engineer, Ray Siebert, during the making of the 2016 Disney film *The Finest Hours*. One hour of the movie was carefully curated to excerpt the most poignant and challenging leadership moments while the tanker was aground and during the rescue. Cadets were later asked to interpret those key moments through the actions of the two protagonists, engraining the lessons in the future leaders' minds for the next fifty years. A similar program with the cadet class of 2027 will continue during the summer of 2025.

A ceremonial model of the CG36500 on display at the Chatham Bar's Inn during the seventieth anniversary ceremonies for the February 18, 1952 rescue of thirty-two seamen from the SS *Pendleton*. *Authors' collection.*

CG36500 Retires

In a twist of fate, the Orleans Historical Society, now renamed the Centers for Culture and History in Orleans, is creating a museum where the venerable CG36500 *Pendleton* rescue boat will be available to the public year-round. Housing the wooden boat in a climate-controlled venue will reduce its exposure to the elements since the craft had been in the water previously. It is thought that being part of a museum will also limit the number and type of volunteers needed and reduce recurring maintenance costs. Fittingly, the museum's name will be the Ocean Rescue Museum of Cape Cod.[95] Jack would have loved that! And Bernie would, too.

Chapter 13

RECOGNIZING AN ENDURING LEGEND

One year after Jack retired, his friend Bernie Webber, the hero of the famous 1952 rescue of thirty-two crewmen from the sinking oil tanker *Pendleton*, died in January 2009, as noted earlier.

Following services in May on Cape Cod, Master Chief Petty Officer of the Coast Guard Skip Bowen devised a concept to name the new fleet of 154-foot fast response cutters (FRCs) after enlisted Coast Guard heroes. He did so on the return flight to Washington from Cape Cod, where Bowen and then Commandant Thad Allen attended funeral services for Bernie Webber. Webber was credited with leading a crew of four who saved thirty-two merchant seamen from the foundering oil tanker *Pendleton* during a February 18, 1952 nor'easter. Webber coxswained the acclaimed motor lifeboat CG36500, onto which the merchant seamen scrambled before the hulk of the *Pendleton* turned over and sank. In 2007, the Coast Guard ranked its top ten rescues of all time, and the *Pendleton* rescue was no. 3, behind only Hurricane Katrina and the 1980 *Prinsendam* cruise ship rescues, making Webber's rescue the greatest small boat rescue in service history.

Bowen told Commandant Allen, "If the cutters were named for heroes who started their careers in the enlisted ranks, it would ensure that lesser known, but very important Coast Guardsmen would be remembered and honored."[96] Almost to the day three years later, the first Sentinel-class fast response cutter named for Bernie Webber slid off the ways in Louisiana and was duly christened in Miami a short time later.

Downey shares a moment with the Coast Guard's Ancient Aviator Chief Peter MacDougall. *Brian Tague.*

Since then, a coordinated effort to get one of the new 154-foot-long fast response cutters named for Master Chief John "Jack" Downey has been in play, but the naming board at Coast Guard HQ has deferred a decision—"New England's and the Coast Guard's first Ancient Keeper had not been part of a singular, big, flashy rescue or a defining moment of personal heroism and leadership," explained a few in the know.

Has the standard for what our former service determined "heroes" been redefined? One can question why and how more contemporary "heroes," including the service's first female electrician and radio operator and the first Hawaiian World War II master chief electrician, could have a hero cutter namesake but not Downey? If being the first in anything is the standard, then Downey's nomination package should be adjusted to include his service-altering firsts. It's not fair to question the contemporary hero's worthiness, but Downey, like many modern-day heroes, did much more for his and the Coast Guard people than his noteworthy operational lifesaving exploits belied.

Downey was believed to be the first to engage the United Kingdom's Royal Naval Lifeboat Institution (RNLI) to obtain cold weather protective suits for his people at his station, the first to make recommendations as part of a 2001 MISHAP Analysis Board that fully funded all cold weather boat forces' units with immersion suits for every sailor, the first unit to host a

The "Ancients" at Downey's retirement ceremony. *Brian Tague.*

fishing vessel safety forum in New England in the early 1990s, the first to create a formal 2003 operational risk management safety standards (Green-Amber-Red) for District One boat forces, likely the first enlisted person to transition from the reserves to active duty (taking a demotion from senior chief to chief in doing so) and the Coast Guard's first Ancient Keeper in the mold of fellow icon and rescuer Joshua James.

Master Chief Jack Downey, the Coast Guard's first Ancient Keeper, is a hero by any definition, past or present.

Downey, who, along with his crews, was credited with saving more than 700 lives during 5,000 rescues—3,500 of which with his direct involvement—is more than qualified to have a cutter named for him based on sheer numbers of operational rescues, longevity of service and commitment to the Coast Guard history during and after retirement, as well as his impact on enlisted boat force's risk and safety protocols. By any measure, including "firsts," he was a respected leader, loved and cherished by many who will stand on his shoulders for decades to come.

The Coast Guard has plans to build as many as seventy-one Webber-class cutters, with fifty-eight already launched. So, there are still opportunities for a Downey FRC namesake or another class cutter namesake or a facility named for New England's legend. But who are some of the other FRCs named for besides the *Pendleton*'s Chief Warrant Officer Webber?

CAPTAIN JOSHUA JAMES

One rescuer every Coast Guardsman knows and respects is Captain Joshua James from the Hull, Massachusetts lifesaving station. James, the inspiration for the Ancient Keeper award that Downey received, was a rescuer for sixty years from the age of fifteen until his death at age seventy-five, when he died performing a rescue. The U.S. Life-Saving Service (USLSS), one of the Coast Guard's predecessor organizations, acknowledged his rescue acumen and first appointed him a Keeper at age sixty-two, six years beyond the age limit for similar appointments.

The Humane Society of the Commonwealth of Massachusetts and the USLSS both bestowed multiple lifesaving medals on James during his tenure as Keeper of the Hull Lifesaving Station.

Downey presents a gift of a portrait of Captain Joshua James to the Coast Guard's Ancient Mariner, Gold Badge, Vice Admiral Papp. *Brian Tague.*

Arguably one of James's most significant rescues and the no. 5 overall among the top ten Coast Guard rescues chronicled in a 2007 summary occurred near the Hull Lifesaving Station over a two-day period in October 25–26, 1888. During that forty-eight-hour period, Keeper James and "his crew by their zealous and unswerving work, rescued some twenty-eight people from five different vessels during a great storm. In addition to the number of individuals rescued, the number of vessels involved, the weather conditions and the duration of their efforts, James and his crew conducted differing types of rescues which included the employment of the beach apparatus and rescue by boat. For their versatility, endurance, skill and dedication, James and his crew were awarded Gold Lifesaving Medals."[97]

While no other modern era–specific rescuer can compare to Joshua James, one can consider it fair to examine other FRC name sakes past and present.

Contemporary Changes Since the Naming Board's Denial

At some point, the HQ naming board took on more expansive definitions of eligible heroes than when Thad Allen and Skip Bowen took that flight back to D.C. from Bernie Webber's 2009 funeral. Appropriately, the board began considering and naming FRCs for several important luminaries in Coast Guard history who have made indelible, positive impacts on service heritage and history. They all are heroes.

Melvin Bell

According to the spring 2024 edition of the National Coast Guard Museum magazine, "Bell distinguished himself during WWII by transmitting the first warning messages to military installations in Pearl Harbor on the morning of December 7, 1941, when the Japanese attacked. He continued to prove instrumental throughout the war as he helped break enemy codes leading to numerous victories, including the Battle of Midway and in an operation to break up a Nazi espionage network in New York City. ETCM Bell became the first Pacific Islander to achieve the rank of Chief Petty Officer and the first master chief electronics technician and first master chief petty officer of color."[98] Bell's nomination and cutter naming are appropriate, given that he could be likened to a modern-day Paul Revere and given his extraordinary codebreaking contributions at a pivotal time during a world war.

Myrtle Hazard

The Coast Guard recognized its first female enlisted member and the only woman to serve in the Coast Guard during World War I with a cutter naming in May 2020 with the thirty-ninth FRC homeported in Key West, Florida. Hazard became the Coast Guard's first female wartime radio operator and the first woman to hold electrician's status. Hazard answered an ad for telegraphers and reported to Coast Guard Headquarters for an interview, but she was quickly dismissed because the service would not have programs for women until 1942. On her way out from the disappointing appointment, she ran into future Commandant Russell Waesche, who immediately recognized her capabilities and hired her. The Coast Guard had no uniforms for women and asked her to choose and develop her own service attire.[99]

Olivia Juliet Hooker

The first African American woman to wear a Coast Guard uniform, Seaman Hooker, enlisted later in life out of a sense of patriotism in the face of discrimination. She completed basic training in April 1945 and went on to attend yeoman school in Manhattan Beach, New York, graduating as a petty officer. Her first assignment was at the Coast Guard Personnel Separation Center in Boston, where she spent most of her time out processing guardsmen who were returning from war and returning to civilian life.

She served her country with distinction and then returned to civilian life and used her GI Bill benefits to receive both master's and doctorate degrees. According to the Coast Guard Historian's website, "Throughout her life, Olivia Hooker was a leader in civic, community, cultural and educational organizations, including the NAACP, her local White Plains Child Daycare Association, Westchester Visiting Nurses Services, and several other organizations. She also served as a consultant on minority issues at Fordham University and as a youth counselor and certified lay speaker in the United Methodist Church. In 2014, Dr. Hooker expressed her own philosophy of service to others: 'It's not about you or me; it's about what we can give to this world.'"[100]

Downey's Involvement in Rescues Big and Small

While Downey didn't have that "one big rescue" to his credit, he found a way to be involved in many major search and rescue (SAR) cases over parts of five decades. And he distinguished himself in ways that more than satisfy more contemporary lenses for cutter naming.

Fishing Vessel General *(1970)*

The first official record of Downey being acknowledged for his proficiency in SAR came via an official letter from the chief of SAR in 1970 from the First Coast Guard District in Boston. Letters like this were unusual, especially from his boss's boss's boss. During what started as a routine April 21 underway training mission in a Station Point Judith forty-foot motor lifeboat, Downey, just two years into a fourteen-year reserve assignment that would see him rise through the ranks from seaman (E3) to senior chief boatswain's mate (E8), was a second class (E5) underway as the rescue boat coxswain. He received a relayed call for help from the fishing vessel (F/V) *General*. At 10:35 a.m., Downey and his crew were six miles south off Weekapaug Inlet, Rhode Island, when the report came in of a mariner with severe abdominal pain. The training mission had quickly transitioned to a real-life SAR case.

Immediately vectoring the forty-foot rescue craft toward the *General*, Downey quickly began to talk the master of the fishing vessel through several medical instructions. By 11:15 a.m., the distressed mariner had been safely transferred from the *General* in five-foot seas. Within minutes, the victim went into cardiac arrest and required lifesaving CPR as Downey drove the boat to the Galilee Pier area, where an ambulance awaited the mariner.

Six months later, Downey received a personal letter of congratulations from Chief of SAR Captain William Ellis for the First Coast Guard District, which read, in part, "Your alertness, quick thinking, and quick actions in saving this man's life is commended. I extend to you my congratulations and 'Well Done!'"[101]

Motor Vessel Sea Comet *(1973)*

On May 19, 1973, the ferry *Sea Comet*, which had been converted into a charter boat, overturned seven miles south of Point Judith, Rhode Island, spilling thirty-three passengers and crew into forty-eight-degree Atlantic waters. The eleven survivors who were rescued by Good Samaritan civilian craft, Downey and his crews, navy boats and rescue helicopters gave conflicting reports about the cause of the accident. Some indicated, "Apparently there were too many people on one side and the boat started to list and take on water. The captain told people to move away from that side, and everyone ran to the other side, causing the boat to capsize. It apparently began sinking stern first."[102]

The Blizzard of 1978

Downey always maintained his Rhode Island home to provide stability for his family, even though he was assigned either permanently or temporarily to multiple New England cutters, boats and stations. His proximity to the Station Point Judith often proved the bane of those who served under his leadership with occasional, unexpected visits by the officer in charge, intent on making sure that the unit was performing according to his high standards. It also enabled him to fill in for his shipmates when they had family emergencies or when harsh New England weather precluded travel.

Over the three-day period of February 5–7, 1978, in what has become known as the Blizzard of 1978, record-breaking snows in Boston and Providence totaling twenty-seven inches kept residents and rescuers house-bound for days. The storm featured unusual "thunder snow," hurricane-force winds up to 111 miles an hour and heavy icing conditions that contributed to hazardous road conditions and downed power lines. Fourteen people died on I-95 when mounting snowdrifts trapped them in their idling vehicles, and many had to be rescued by skiers and snowmobilers. In Downey's Point Judith end-of-tour award, he was cited for standing the watch for others who were unable to make their way to the station and ensuring that the Coast Guard was ready to assist mariners under the worst conditions.

Motor Vessel Quonset *(August 9, 1980)*

The ferry *Quonset* departed the Galilee, Rhode Island piers with 442 passengers en route to the Block Island tourist destination on August 9, 1980. The ferry soon lost power and was adrift, headed for an allision with nearby piers or the breakwater. Downey and his crews quickly acted as tugs alongside the stricken motor vessel and brought the vessel back to safe harbor for repairs. The headline read, "Ferry with 442 Aboard Loses Steering Near Pier; Coast Guard Saves the Day."[103]

Motor Vessel Pilgrim Belle *(1985)*

Master Chief Downey took over as the officer in charge of the very busy station at Woods Hole, Massachusetts, in 1984. Large ferries with up to 1,500 passengers would routinely sail in his area of responsibility, transiting to and from the nearby tourist destinations of Martha's Vineyard and Nantucket.

At 4:20 p.m. on July 16, 1985, the 196-foot-long, 96-gross-ton ferry *Pilgrim Belle* ran aground on Sow and Pigs Reef, Vineyard Sound, Massachusetts. The master of the vessel, noting that the *Pilgrim Belle* took on a 5- to 7-degree port list and upon being informed that his ship was flooding in the crew's quarters, storeroom and lazarette, coordinated with the ship's designer through Coast Guard Station Woods Hole. The designer advised that the storeroom must be kept dry, and after making a quick assessment, the captain immediately called for the evacuation of all eighty-four passengers and sixteen crew members. Eight crew and one shipyard representative remained with the ferry.[104]

Coast Guard Station Woods Hole coordinated the one hundred evacuees to be transferred to the nearby fishing vessel *Fare Lady*, as well as one of *Pilgrim Belle*'s motor launches and local recreational boats, and brought to Cuttyhunk Island and Base Woods Hole. The *Pilgrim Belle* did not sink but suffered $357,000 damage and was returned to service on August 31, 1985.[105] The NTSB later determined that the master of the vessel failed to actively navigate his vessel.

JFK Jr. (1999)

On July 16, 1999, John F. Kennedy Jr., his wife and her sister crashed in a small airplane seven miles southwest of Martha's Vineyard, Massachusetts. The initial crash location was ambiguous because Kennedy flew using visual flight rules from New Jersey to Massachusetts, and radar tracking data took a few days to sort out. While no survivors were rescued, Downey was the first Group Woods Hole search professional to point rescuers to the approaches to Martha's Vineyard. This early action centered the search, enabling critical flotsam and jetsam to be retrieved and analyzed by NOAA using oil-tracking technologies, further focusing the later underwater recovery efforts. This ultimately minimized the time family members waited to honor their loved ones in ceremonies.

EgyptAir 990 (1999)

Two and a half short months after the JFK Jr. crash, on October 31, 1999, a New York to Cairo EgyptAir commercial flight was taken over and crashed by a relief pilot sixty miles south of Nantucket, Rhode Island, killing all 217 passengers and crew. The relief pilot wrested control from the regular pilot, eventually shutting off the fuel to all the plane's engines and causing the crash. Downey and his cutter *Hammerhead* crew were extolled for their professionalism in providing the operational commander with on-scene briefings and recovering and transporting wreckage and human remains to the Davisville, Rhode Island Recovery and Reconstruction site. His efforts were specifically heralded by the incident commander in providing "closure for the families and the public and facilitating the NTSB's accident investigation."[106]

Fishing Vessel Seldom Home *(2005)*

The master chief's last formally recognized rescue occurred in 2005 while he was the officer in charge of the *Hammerhead*, an eighty-two-foot Protector-class cutter that he had previously commanded on two occasions. His fourth Coast Guard commendation citation read, "Exhibiting superior judgment and seamanship skills, Master Chief Downey expertly led his crew in the Rescue and Assistance (R&A) of the Fishing Vessel *Seldom Home*, 17 miles south of Nantucket, Massachusetts. Arriving on scene, *Hammerhead*'s R&A

Above: Senior Chiefs McClay and Lucey and the third Ancient Keeper, CWO Guthlein, at the First Annual Jack Downey Boat Forces Unit Awards, Portsmouth, New Hampshire, May 2024. *Authors' collection.*

Left: Judith Downey receives an accolade from a senior Coast Guard official at the First Annual Jack Downey Boat Forces Unit Awards, Portsmouth, New Hampshire, May 2024. *Authors' collection.*

team transferred two dewatering pumps to the disabled vessel and had them running within minutes, controlled the flooding, ultimately saving the vessel and three-person crew."[107]

A Significant Acknowledgement

The Office of Boat Forces at Coast Guard Headquarters announced the establishment of the Master Chief Jack Downey Unit Awards in December 2023 and the names of the first recipients on March 14, 2024. The four Downey Unit Awards were designed to acknowledge "recipients who possess the strongest combination of Mission Performance, Leadership and Partnerships, Community Outreach, Readiness and Safety."[108]

At least one hundred people attended a moving ceremony at Station Portsmouth Harbor, New Hampshire, on May 22, 2024, to honor the first four Downey Award recipient units on a beautiful sunny day at one of the service's most iconic stations. Most of the Downey family members mentioned in this book were present, with Master Chief Downey's daughter Jennifer providing a beautiful testimonial to her father as a family man and a dedicated rescuer and mentor to many.

Way Forward

As of this writing, Master Chief Downey's name remains under active consideration by the Coast Guard's naming board for one of the future fast response cutters. The Coast Guard should reconsider his name because its original denial was based on the master chief not having a seminal rescue like his mentor Bernie Webber's 1952 *Pendleton* rescue. Its criteria have obviously morphed and expanded to be inclusive and considerate of an amplified definition of what a hero is in contemporary times.

In 2009, despite Bowen and Commandant Allen's advocacy to name the FRCs after enlisted heroes, the naming board voted the idea down. It already had an approved list of cutter names linked to the words *sentinel* and *guardian*. Master Chief Bowen, according to the Coast Guard Historian's oral history, "thought that it was a missed opportunity that the Coast Guard was naming its new FRCs using variations of the words Sentinel and Guardian, and not naming them after heroes like Webber."[109]

Bowen was undeterred and approached then Vice-Commandant Dave Pekoske in February 2010, asking him to intervene. Pekoske overruled the naming board's objections and opined, "This was a leadership decision, respectful of the board, with intent to celebrate our history, inspire our workforce and honor our heroes and their families. Naming cutters after things or adjectives doesn't do nearly as much in further developing a culture of leadership, character, and selfless service."[110]

It's time for today's Coast Guard leadership to reconsider the naming board's decision in the same way they did in 2010 to honor New England's and Rhode Island's premier rescuer and multigenerational inspirational leader with a cutter naming. It's our hope that the naming board will reconsider its decision and appropriately honor Downey with a cutter or major facility naming.

Appendix 1

SIMPLE WISDOM ENDURES

By Captain W. Russell Webster, USCG (Ret.)

Three years after the master chief's death, one can marvel at how much we didn't know, how many people Downey influenced and how his memories and actions continue to give me and others direction. I was preparing a big speech for the National Coast Guard Search and Rescue conference in St. Louis, April 9–12, 2024, and in developing my talk about a phenomenon called "normalcy bias," the "why" behind complacency and the silent killer in search and rescue decision-making, I used some of Jack's simple wisdom to convey a most complex concept to an important and influential audience of the seventy most senior search and rescue professionals in the Coast Guard.

I remember how driven Jack always was about pursuing the truth and taking an operational lesson to the finish line to make a difference. He did that when he was part of my team that investigated the deaths of two guardsmen during the March 23, 2001 Niagara MISHAP investigation. Two Coasties perished in cold Lake Ontario waters on a nighttime law enforcement mission when the coxswain deviated from the float plan and the boat overtopped a wave, burying its bow and flipping the crew into the chilly waters.

Master Chief held fast to his conviction afterward that local station personnel needed new tools for risk management. He did so because he knew that if he didn't push every possible button, whether it was a relationship or the development of new policies on behalf of his beloved service, he couldn't sleep at night.

In the 2001 Niagara case, he saw an opportunity to help other Coasties and their families to avoid the tragic outcome that can come from ignoring preventable risk in an unforgiving environment. He pursued this with dogged intensity, melding elements of the Auxiliary's Team Coordination Team (TCT) risk management training with common sense know-how and produced the first functional Green Amber Red boat forces risk management program in the form a District One (Northeast) operational risk management instruction on April 1, 2003.

And there I was in St. Louis, at the Coast Guard's 2024 national SAR conference, pitching solutions to an endemic watchstander problem with normalcy bias, a condition that affects all of us when faced with ambiguous problems. I had been working this issue for the better part of fifteen years. Normalcy bias causes us to think, "Everything will be fine," when faced with ambiguous and difficult circumstances and that's mostly all right, except when we are making decisions on behalf of troubled mariners. Then, in the worst of SAR cases, where ambiguity is high, watchstanders make decisions not based on the facts, but rather on past cases that are somewhat close to the current circumstances and allow the tension and anxiety of ambiguity to be resolved and be "normal" again.

The key to my talk was to promote a new model in the SAR command centers that values a new decision-making risk management model featuring a new form of positive tension and a victim advocate who can disrupt bias toward "normal" with a measure of healthy conflict. I had done the best job I could with the presentation and was searching for a great example of something the audience of SAR leaders can take from the talk and make a difference immediately. And then I recalled something the master chief did during every officer in charge (OIC) review panel.

No matter how well prepared an OIC candidate appeared to be, Jack would always ask, "Are you sure about that?" When I recalled his practice of simple wisdom, I realized this was the "silver bullet" for my presentation. Something so basic and actionable that mirrored the healthy, respectful conflict I was advocating in my new SAR decision-making model. Remembering even the best-prepared candidates' reactions to the master chief's question solidified my resolve to honor him and use his OIC panel question as a takeaway to the senior SAR representatives.

It also steeled me to keep pressing all buttons necessary to continue my advocacy for healthier SAR decision-making protocols for the Coast Guard he loved, we loved, together. I miss the master chief, but I'm sure he knows we're standing on his shoulders. I've become the dog with a bone for the Boat Forces people who quietly do the important work of saving ten people each day, all across America.

Appendix 2

A LEGACY OF THREE

There's an oft-repeated leadership axiom that today's leaders "stand on the shoulders" of those leaders who came before them, inspired them and, in part, made them who they became. No other leaders represent this tried-and-true thought and owe more to Master Chief Downey than these three high-achieving acolytes.

Senior Chief Gordon "Gordie" McClay, U.S. Coast Guard (Ret.)

Senior Chief Gordon "Gordie" McClay qualified in all four major officer in charge (OIC) certification categories, including Aids to Navigation, Afloat and Ashore and Multi-Mission Afloat and Ashore. This is in addition to being utility boat and motor lifeboat (MLB) qualified and heavy weather coxswain qualified, retiring after serving as OIC at an MLB station. In his twenty-eight-year career, McClay credited Master Chief Downey for showing him the way from his early days at Woods Hole as a boatswain's mate third class, all the way to encouraging McClay to join Downey as his executive petty officer at Station Brant Point, where Master Chief helped him attain the rank of chief petty officer. McClay retired in 2012 after a distinguished career in the Coast Guard and still resides with his family in Plymouth, Massachusetts.

Throughout his career, McClay often found himself asking, "What would Master Chief do?" Master Chief had a unique way of balancing empathy with authority, teaching that leadership wasn't just about giving orders—it was about earning trust and inspiring others to achieve their best. One moment that stands out occurred during the hurricane preparations at Station Brant Point in 1996. In the face of chaos, Master Chief's calm, decisive leadership set the tone for the entire crew and showed McClay what it truly meant to lead by example.

Master Chief's wisdom often came through in his simple but profound phrases. One of his favorites, "Eye the wind," was a constant refrain during ship maneuvers. While it was sound advice for navigating tricky waters, it also carried a deeper meaning. "Eye the wind" became a metaphor for life, a reminder to understand the external forces—both physical and metaphorical—that could impact one's course. Master Chief taught that success wasn't about fighting these forces but working with them to achieve one's goals.

McClay carried this lesson into every aspect of his life. Whether navigating a literal storm or a personal challenge, he still hears Master Chief's voice reminding him to "Eye the wind." The phrase encapsulated so much of Master Chief's wisdom—practical, profound and grounded in the realities of both the sea and life. Even years after leaving the Coast Guard, Master Chief's words continue to guide him.

Beyond his technical expertise, Master Chief's mentorship prepared McClay for the human aspects of leadership—how to listen, guide and earn respect. Master Chief often emphasized the value of humility in leadership, a principle that McClay continues to practice to this day. As McClay reflects on his journey, he considers himself fortunate to have been one of Master Chief's acolytes. Downey's influence extended far beyond their time together, shaping McClay's approach to leadership as a Coast Guardsman, father, husband and community member. Master Chief's legacy lives on in the countless lives he touched, including McClay's.

Chief Warrant Officer Tom Guthlein, USCG (Ret.)

Chief Warrant Officer Tom Guthlein's three-decade mentorship and friendship continued until Downey's death. He recalled his first experience with the master chief fondly. "Chatham was a successful tour. I liked Master

Chief because he was a straight shooter, even though some of the lessons were difficult to accept at the time. You always knew where you stood with him. He always had the best for you and the Coast Guard in mind, even though at the time, you might not see it. I learned a lot, about myself and the Coast Guard. We worked prototype projects together, like dry suits for the crews, and that made me see how visionary he was about the future of the Guard, its personnel and their equipment. He was always there for his people and to do the right thing for the right reason. If you weren't big enough to challenging yourself, he'd challenge you and you wouldn't even be aware of it. By the time you were aware of it, it was too late. You were already treading water neck deep."

In his career, CWO Guthlein qualified as a coxswain, heavy weather coxswain, surfman and surfman instructor. He served as the executive petty officer of one multi-mission unit and officer in charge of three multi-mission, motor lifeboat boat units. He became the first motor lifeboat instructor to serve from New England (with shallow water experience), served five years on a Headquarters Utility Boat Standardization Team and won the David H. Jarvis Inspirational Leadership Award in 2005, which "recognizes the Coast Guard Officer who has made outstanding contributions to the high standards of competence and leadership traditions in the Coast Guard." Following in Downey's footsteps, he became the Coast Guard's third Ancient Keeper in 2009.[111]

At the time of this writing, he is the deputy director for Rhode Island's Emergency Management Agency (RIEMA). In that capacity, he assists the director in decision-making and determining the current and future operational planning efforts of the agency to assume the duties of the director in their absence, answering directly to the governor. Mr. Guthlein "paid it forward" and has counseled many future leaders throughout their careers, most notably his son, Joshua, who is a lieutenant on active duty with the Coast Guard.

Senior Chief Sheila Lucey

Senior Chief Sheila Lucey retired in 2007 after a twenty-four-year career in the Coast Guard. Under Master Chief's guidance, she became the first female surfman in the U.S. Coast Guard. Downey was "a second father to me and a brilliant mentor and leader in all aspects of life. Whether prosecuting search and rescue cases or leading and guiding people, Master Chief set

Downey and Senior Chief McClay at Sheila Lucey's retirement at Station Brant Point, May 2007. *Brian Tague.*

the standard and the ultimate example. He was a master at reading and understanding people and was the smartest person in the room, no matter what room he was in. He commanded your respect. His intolerance for foolishness ensured that you always knew where you stood with him. His leadership style which blended confidence, decisiveness, humility, quick wit, and an overabundance of common sense is the perfect recipe for an exceptional leader. He was very best. Truly the GOAT."

Downey influenced her entire Coast Guard career, and his influence extended past her retirement. He advised her to get into Aids to Navigation in the Coast Guard so she would be well versed in more of the Coast Guard's missions. He prepared her for challenging roles, including as first lieutenant on a 110-foot patrol boat, officer in charge of an Aids to Navigation team and officer in charge of a small boat station, eventually transitioning to a civilian role as assistant harbormaster on Nantucket. From there, she rose to become harbormaster, leading a team of sixty lifeguards and twenty dock staff and boat crews throughout the summer. Her "second father" in and out of uniform taught her many practical lessons—"many that I pass on to my crews and lifeguards now. I think we're all better for it." Lucey's mentorship has been recognized for helping several youth matriculate to higher education opportunities at the Massachusetts Maritime Academy and the U.S. Coast Guard Academy and enlisting in the Coast Guard or U.S. Navy. Master Chief Downey's leadership has had a ripple effect, positively shaping the lives of countless others—those who still wear the uniform as well as many who don't.

Appendix 3

SOUL OF THE SERVICE AWARD

Downey earned the Soul of the Service Award for his four decades of faithful and unwavering service.

OFFICE OF BOAT FORCES AWARD

Presented to BMCM John "Jack" Downey
First Coast Guard District, Command Master Chief

In great appreciation of your selfless dedication and unwavering commitment to Coast Guard Boat Forces. The leadership and training that you have provided throughout your 41 years of service has had a profound impact on those who have served with you and those who will follow.

20 June 2008
Jeffrey L. Wheeler
Acting Chief, Office of Boat Forces

Appendix 4

A GRANDSON'S TESTIMONIAL

"Sea Glass"
by Jayson Sanford

The clock reads 6:15 in the morning. As I raise myself upright on your couch from a peaceful sleep, I can start to see the sun peeking through the curtains from the floor to ceiling windows. I quietly tip toe past my younger brother who is still asleep on the other couch to go use the bathroom. I come back to the living room to see Justyn awake now watching T.V. I snuggle back onto the couch as he flips through the channels to find something for us to watch. We both wait in excitement for you to make your way down the hallway to get the day started.

As we hear your bedroom door open and your footsteps approaching, we both perk up from our couches waiting to see your face. "Yo, what are you doing," you ask, as we both respond back to you, "Yo, what are you doing." You make your way into the living room and sit next to Justyn to watch T.V. with us. After relaxing for a bit, we start to pull ourselves together to head out of the house for the morning. We gather into the blue Nissan and make our way to Dunkin' Donuts. You order your usual…hot coffee with cream and a box of munchkins for all of us. You drive us along your favorite route as you drink your coffee while Justyn and I enjoy the water views. You park the car along the sea wall and we all start walking toward the beach. As we hit the sand, Justyn and I run to the water quick to see the waves, then we run back to you to start our adventure. From where we stand the beach looks like it is never ending, going miles and miles. At this moment the game begins.

We would spread out a little trying to cover as much ground as possible in search of finding sea glass. With your coffee cup empty by now, whenever someone would find a piece of sea glass, we would run to you and use the cup to hold the so-called treasure. Brown, Clear, Green, Blue, Red of all shapes and sizes were scattered across the beach. To us, red was the rarest find of any piece of sea glass. Pretty much if you were the one to find red, you won the game. We would always fill your coffee cup to the brim with sea glass, having to turn to filling our shorts pockets because we would find so much. No other beach could compare to the amount of sea glass on yours. Mom would take us back home to Falmouth after the weekend, and we would try to search for sea glass on the Cape beaches to only find a couple of pieces. Looking back, it makes me think that it wasn't the good luck of the beach that made us find so much sea glass; however, it was your presence being on that sand that gave us good fortune.

We would make that long walk back to your blue Nissan full of joy and relaxation. Those summer weekends spent with you were some of my best memories, and I will never forget those moments on the beach with you searching for sea glass. It will be a tradition I pass on to my son. I never realized it in the moment, but as I grow older you were teaching me how to be patient. How to be focused. How to appreciate the environment around you. How to bond with one another. How to tell good stories. How to start the day early and on the right foot. How to love your family. How…to search for sea glass.

Love you, Pop.

Appendix 5

"EN VOYAGE"

Read by MCPO Downey's five children at his funeral.

There's a ship sailing on to a harbor,
To a haven of comfort and rest.
It's a ship of God's fashion and making.
And its voyage by him will be best.
It departed with silence and beauty,
With the Master, Himself, in command.
As with dignity truly majestic
It sailed out of sight of land.
There will always clear skies above it.
There will always be calmness below,
There will never be storms to harass it,
For the Master is on it, you know.
And His wisdom will carry it safely
To the port of His infinite peace,
Where the light of His love will protect it
With a blessing that will never cease.
You have watched it sail onward and outward,
With a tear of regret in your eye.
For a loved one was sailing upon it,
And there's grief when saying goodbye.
But your years would be tears of rejoicing,

And your heart would be happy and free.
If you could look for only a moment
On that ship that is sailing to sea.
For the one you have loved is at leisure,
With no worry or trouble or care.
There's contentment beyond understanding,
In the way God's passengers fare.
And you'd know from your own observation.
That the sailing was joyful, not grim.
For it means a new life and new living.
And a sweet, closer contact with Him.
Oh, the solace there is the knowledge,
Life is life and it will always be.
And it's simply a change of direction,
When we sail on HIS ship out to sea.
And the tears that we shed for our loved ones
Are in truth shed for us left behind.
For it hurts to give up to the Master.
Tho we know He is gentle and kind.
So, believe in His great and good wisdom,
Trust in Him as you patiently wait.
On His ship God is ever the pilot
And the one you have loved is the mate.

Appendix 6

REMEMBRANCES

Downey's legacy may best be remembered by the many thoughtful words of wisdom that his colleagues from the Boston Chief's Mess bestowed on him upon retiring (following is only a small sampling).

"I always thought Jack's biggest legacy was that he was never retired on Active duty. He mentored people like Sheila Lucey and Gordie McClay and thousands of other people long after he retired."[112]

"Profound influence on the lives of countless Coast Guard men and women, knowledge, skill and sense of humor."[113]

"Never worked with you directly but worked with others that did, and the true sense of a leader is when people learn from you secondhand."[114]

"A chief is strong, honest, available, wise, keeps a watchful eye. I've learned so much about being a chief from you that it's difficult for me to think of a CG without you."[115]

"The service will never be able to repay you. You've been given more privilege and responsibility than any other enlisted person in the world, and you did not abuse it."[116]

"The power of influence via association. Proofing with the 'what if' test. Tom Guthlein taught me to maintain the highest standard and never accept half-measures. You are a true and eternal member of the CG heroes."[117]

"In a world where the chiefs don't have the power they once had you have remained steadfast. Through your leadership your willingness to accept nothing but the best will carry on for years to come. Thank you for your mentorship and being a hard ass to make your peers dig deep down within themselves to reach higher and simply not settle for just getting by."[118]

Departing from the excerpts, included here is MCPO Kyle Takakjian's complete communique because it includes aspects of other submissions that were similar but not as complete:

"I spoke about you, and the conclusion we came to was that of all the things you have passed to us, the one that stands out the most—was that you taught us how to keep ourselves out of trouble. Not in the sense of the law, but the practical stuff that would keep our crews and us safe from harm.

When I first worked for you, I couldn't understand why you were being such a pain in the ass about all the little stuff. But as time went on—and you started to spend time with us underway, I began to realize that the details, preparation, learning and skills developed made all of us better engineers, crewman and boat drivers. Most of the stuff wouldn't matter on a calm, sunny afternoon. But it would matter when the weather got rough, the bar was nasty, and the equipment wasn't as reliable or modern as some of the stuff in use today. I think you were building people who knew the importance of 'Operational Excellence' before the phrase was adopted by our boss.

Additionally, you always emphasize humor, having some fun and preserving our history—and that last part, especially today helps to give our young folks a sense of purpose—that way to bridge the past to our future."[119]

Passing the Torch
by BMCS Colleen McCarthy

A time has come when the torch will be passed,
A decorated Master Chief will lay ashore after 40 years amassed.
Many will gather to celebrate with much appreciation,
And bear witness to the time-honored tradition at Point Judith Station.
  This Boatswain's Mate will retire Active Service to his country,
Embraced by small boats ashore and cutters at sea.
A Rhode Island native who enlisted in 1966
Will pass the Joshua James torch which honors Boat Forces Leadership.
  An Officer In Charge, Surfman, Cutter Man, and Gold Badge Chief,
Accomplishments in so many milestones that only so many reach.
An Ancient Keeper who has spent a career along the New England coast,
Will leave behind a legacy that is appropriate to boasts.
  A service with a heritage at the "Point" in the Ocean State,
Will end so honorably after many years as a legacy Boatswains Mate.
Master Chief Downey, a lifesaver that rescued many in the Northeast chill,
Will pass the converted torch to the Bos'n from the Station at Castle Hill.
  Fair Winds and Following Seas as you make your transition,
With sincere thanks for paving the way for all that marvel at your ambition.
On behalf of the crew at the Woods Hole Station,
I express my deepest gratitude for your service to our nation.[120]

Appendix 7

THE RETIREMENT FLAG PASSING CEREMONY

Upon retirement, Downey received his Flag, the passing initiated by his grandsons Jayson and Justyn. A process of passing a folded flag from person to person, starting with the lowest-ranking person until it reaches Downey. Before being passed each time, the passing ends with a hand salute at each station. Each station documented a window of Downey's career.

I am the flag of the United States of America. My name is Old Glory.

I fly atop the world tallest buildings.

I stand within America's halls of justice.

I fly majestically over the greatest institutions of learning.

I was there when Jack Downey joined the Coast Guard in November 1966. And I was there in Cape May, New Jersey, when Seamen Apprentice Downey graduated Basic Training and reported to the cutter *Casco* and patrolled the North Atlantic on Ocean Station and Search and Rescue assignments.

I stand guard with the greatest military power in the world. I stand for peace, honor, truth and justice. I stand for freedom. I am confident and proud. And I was there when Seaman Downey reported to Coast Guard Air Station Salem, Massachusetts, in March 1968 as a rescue and recovery boat crewman on the 40-foot utility boat for aircraft takeoffs and landings.

When I am flown with my fellow banners, my head is a little higher, my colors a little truer. I bow to no one. And I was there when in September 1968 when BM3 Downey reported to Coast Guard Station Point Judith where he qualified as boat coxswain on the 40-foot Utility Boat and the 44-

Coast Guard Air Station Salem. *USCG photo.*

foot Motor Lifeboat and underwent his first Coast Guard investigation. He wants me to say he was found not guilty.

I am recognized the world over. I am saluted. I am respected. I am loved and I am feared. And I was there in 1970 when BM2 Downey was the coxswain for the medevac of an injured fisherman off the F/V *General*. In 5- to 6-foot seas off Nebraska Shoals, Point Judith, Rhode Island. I was there when the crew successfully resuscitated the unconscious fisherman and saved his life.

I have fought every battle of every war for more than two hundred years. When America fought for freedom, I was there. I was there in World War I, World War II, Korea, Vietnam, the Persian Gulf and Afghanistan. And I was there when BM1 Downey was the boat operations search and rescue instructor for the reserve units throughout southeastern Massachusetts and Rhode Island. I was there when he served as reserve Unit Petty Officer, Training Officer, Boat Coxswain and Officer of the Day at Coast Guard Station Point Judith from 1971 through 1979.

I led sailors. I followed them. I watched over them. They loved me. I was in a small boat in Guadalcanal. And I was there when Chief Boatswain's Mate Downey served as the Officer in Charge of Coast Guard Station Point

Navy League of the United States

The Douglas A. Munro Award
for Inspirational Leadership
and Professional Competence

The United States Coast Guard's only Congressional Medal of Honor recipient displayed supreme leadership when he gave his life while leading a fleet of boats to evacuate a battalion of Marines trapped on a beach at Guadalcanal during World War II. Signalman First Class Douglas A. Munro daringly directed his craft to draw the enemy's fire and shielded the other boats from the constant strafing of machine guns. His courageous efforts made the perilous evacuation successful and saved the lives of many brave men who otherwise would have perished. By his magnificent performance and dauntless devotion to duty this heroic Coast Guardsman exemplified the highest level of leadership and professional competence.

In memory of the lasting inspiration of this great Coast Guardsman, the Navy League of the United States is honored to make this Award in 1990 to:

Senior Chief Boatswain's Mate
John E. Downey, USCG

for outstanding leadership and professional competence in the performance of his duties as Officer-in-Charge at the Chatham, Massachusetts, Coast Guard Station. Senior Chief Downy succeeded in creating harmonious relations between the station and the local community. He significantly improved station crew morale, initiated rigorous search and rescue training programs, and obtained funding for much needed lifesaving craft and equipment. Having evaluated environmental conditions at the station, he implemented an extensive depth-sounding plan. Utilizing a nine-meter Le COMPTE rigid hull inflatable lifeboat, he conducted intensive drills in all weather and surf conditions. Additionally, he established a number of recreational boating safety programs for the community.

Senior Chief Downey's professional competence and dedication to duty are consistent with the finest traditions of the United States Coast Guard.

Presented this 4th day of June, 1990.

Calvin H. Cobb, Jr.
National President

Vice Admiral William F. Rea III, USCG (Ret.)
Chairman, Coast Guard Awards Board

Nicholas Brango
Corporate Secretary

Master Chief Downey's Munro Award citation, July 2006. *Brian Tague.*

Judith, and I sailed with him aboard the Coast guard cutter *Chase*, where he performed migrant operations and drug interdiction and was recognized for saving the ship and her crew during an Underway Replenishment with a Navy ship. I was also there when Chief Downey became the first Officer in Charge of Coast Guard Station Woods Hole where he and his crew responded to over 800 distress calls saving or assisting over 2,000 people, including 108 elderly passengers, from the sinking ship *Pilgrim Belle*, which was taking on water off the coast of Cutty Hunk Island, and the 9 crewmen from the burning Fishing Vessel *Nordic Pride*.

I have been soiled, burned, torn and trampled on in the streets of countries that I have helped to set free. It does not hurt for I am strong. And I was there when Senior Chief Boatswain's Mate Downey received the Douglas A. Munroe Award for inspirational leadership and professional competence. I was also there when Senior Chief Downey and his crew re-established Coast Guard Station Chatham as a designated surf station.

I have been soiled, burned, torn and trampled on in the streets of other countries. And when it is done by those with whom I stand in this great country, it hurts. But I shall overcome for I am strong. And I was there when Master Chief Downey was assigned to Coast Guard Cutter *Hammerhead* as the Officer in Charge after two temporary assignments. I was there when after the attack on America on September 11, 2001, when within forty-eight hours of reassignment to the cutter, he trained his crew and readied the cutter to perform national Security Missions patrolling the harbor security zones surrounding the Statue of Liberty and the United Nations Building in New York Harbor. I was also there when as Officer in Charge of Coast Guard Cutter *Hammerhead* Master Chief Downey and his crew conducted Search and Rescue cases, including the search and recovery of plane crash victims of EgyptAir 990 and numerous living marine resource patrols, conducting boardings within high-threat areas.

And I was there when Master Chief Downey was an instructor at the Command and Operations School, Leadership Development Center, United States Coast Guard Academy, where he instructed over 1,000 cutter commanding and executive officers and over 300 international maritime officers from fifty countries with his students ranging from Seamen to Admirals in collision avoidance skills and the practical application of the Rules of the Road.

And I was there when Master Chief Downey was the First District's Command Master Chief, conveying his career's important lessons and supporting New England's Coast Guard crews and their family members.

Appendix 8

REAR ADMIRAL TIM SULLIVAN'S JUNE 20, 2008 RETIREMENT SPEECH FOR MCPO DOWNEY

Ladies and Gentlemen, good morning. And thank you to Admiral Crea who was kind enough to let me speak for this portion of today's ceremony.

It is now time to focus our attention and attempt to pay proper tribute to a man who has given more than 40 years of his life to our service and country…and fortunately for me, the retirement ceremonies are a bit more informal, so I ask you all to sit back, relax, put your feet up if you can… not you Master Chief…and come along with me as we talk about the great Master Chief Jack Downey….

As the District Command Master Chief, Jack and I have spent a lot of time together, and I've always enjoyed traveling with him. It was fun to awake from an afternoon siesta aboard one of our many Auxiliary Flights to find him ashen faced and gripping the seat for dear life…he's not a big fan of flying.

Also, at the units we'd visit, he was regularly approached by retired Coasties, who greeted him like long lost family. Retired Master Chiefs, Captains, OICs, all greeted him with open arms. They'd often be our age, or slightly older, and I'd ask Jack if he worked for them in the past. And every time his answer would be "No, they were a non-rate when I was OIC at Chatham," or "They were a BM2 out at Brant Point." In fact, I don't think I ever met an Officer in Charge or Executive Petty Officer who Master Chief worked FOR. If there is anyone in the audience who had the "pleasure" of having Jack Downey work for them, officers not included, please raise your hands. Well, we owe you men a round of applause as well because I know, and Master Chief would be the first to say this, that he owes much of his success to all of you.

I noticed a common theme during these trips, however; nearly everyone I talked to, including Federal, State, and Local partners, knew personally, or had worked with, Master Chief Downey at some point.

I had not sailed in New England since 1998 but when I saw his name on the short list of potential Command Master Chiefs, I didn't hesitate for a second to pick up the phone and ask him to take the position. To say the least, his name and reputation precede him well. In fact, his name has become almost lore in New England, and many have even gone so far as to use the term "legend."

Well, I think it may be a little bold for any person to deem another a "legend," but we'll take a look at this.…Our friend Webster says: "*Legend: a story, or body of stories, handed down for generations and popularly believed to have a historical basis.*"

I like this definition, and I will come back to that at the end of this story. But first, it is tradition during these ceremonies for the guest speaker to run through the retiree's assignments and accolades.

However, after 40 years of service, twelve assignments, and countless achievements, by the time I ran through it all, the food would have gone bad. So, with your permission Admiral, and Master Chief, I'll depart a bit from the standard retirement ceremony speech for efficiency while still paying proper tribute to Jack Downey.

And, taking his lead, I will start, "First and foremost" by thanking his wife, Judith, daughters, Jennifer, Heather, and Rebecca. Sons, Shawn and Ryan, and grandchildren, Jayson, Justyn, Tahlia (Tah-lia), D.J., Ava (A-vuh), and Seamus for the support and love you've shown your husband, father, and grandfather over the years. I asked Master Chief if there was something special he'd like me to say to his family. He said there wasn't…but the one thing he appreciated most was that his family always made it easy for him to do this job because of who you were and how you acted. And the cornerstone of that was Judith.

Every one of you sacrificed in your own way so he could continue on in this service. And while it's never easy on anyone to miss anniversaries, birthdays, ballgames, or any of the other important milestones in our lives, your support, understanding, and character ensured that Jack could go out and do this job without worrying about what was going on back at home.

Whether you realize it or not, each of you played a tremendous part in Jack's success and I know he appreciates it every day. So, thank you for Your service and dedication to the Master Chief, your efforts allowed him to serve with all of us.

Now, let's take a boat ride down the career of Master Chief Jack Downey.

Master Chief Jack Downey enlisted in the Coast Guard on November 28th, 1966. By the way, ***I*** was in the 7th grade....

And I know its common at these ceremonies to talk about what things were like the day the retiree entered the service, but instead, I'd like to talk about what hadn't happened yet. And to make this more "interactive," we'll do it with a show of hands. I'm going to say a few things and for our active-duty folks in the audience, please raise your hand if you were in the Coast Guard BEFORE this happened. Ready?

Ok, raise your hand if you were in the Coast Guard...

- Before the Department of Homeland Security (2003)...OK... and keep them up if you were in the Coast Guard...
- Before the Berlin wall came down (1989)
- Before President Reagan (1981)
- Before personal computers (1977)
- Before the Miami Dolphins' undefeated season (1972)
- Before man walked on the moon (July 1969)
- How about when the Coast Guard was part of the Department of Treasury (April 1967)

Ok, I assumed it would end up something close to this. So Master Chief was in the Coast Guard before Neil took his small step...just imagine how much the Coast Guard, and the world, has changed in the last 40 years... and Master Chief was along for the whole ride.

After graduating from boot camp in Cape May New Jersey, this Providence, Rhode Island native returned to New England to sail aboard the CGC *Casco*, a 311-foot cutter homeported in Boston, Massachusetts.

In December 1967, Master Chief married his High School sweetheart, Judith, and the two packed up their things and went right up the road to Air Station Salem, Massachusetts where he...

What???

Do you mean that some of you aren't familiar with Air Station Salem, Massachusetts? Well, then you're in good company because I had never heard of it before either. Apparently, we didn't need runways "back in the day" and simply landed our airplanes right on the water. As a cadet I had a chance to fly the Albatross but they were not only water for landings.

And BM3 Downey served as a ready coxswain in the crash boat who was responsible for responding to emergencies but also had to "clear the runway" of recreational boaters as the planes came in. Sounds like some pretty sweet duty.

In the spring of '68, Master Chief was transferred right here to Station Point Judith. He served as a Coxswain and advanced quickly to BM2. However, the active-duty Coast Guard wasn't what he was looking for at the time, and he transferred to the Reserves in November 1970. A month later, his daughter Jennifer was born followed by Heather in 1973 and Shawn in 1974.

Life was good for Jack, Judith, Jennifer, Heather, and Shawn. Master Chief was a Master Plumber in the area and he spent his one weekend a month and two weeks a year at Station PT Judith. He advanced to Chief Petty Officer in 1975. Yup, that's over 33 years, 28 of which were active duty, that Jack Downey has served as a Chief Petty Officer.

33 years, as a Chief…remarkable.

In 1978, he advanced to Senior Chief Boatswain's Mate and then, in the summer of '79, the twins, Ryan and Rebecca, were born. And life was Really good.

But the sea…she is a relentless mistress. And when the Commanding Officer of Group Woods Hole asked Senior Chief Downey to take Command of Station Point Judith in late 1979, he accepted.

He spent two years at Station PJ and fully integrated back into Active-Duty Service, but in order to do so, he had to take a demotion to Chief Petty Officer…not such a bad thing.

In 1982 the detailer finally took a good look at his resume and decided that the young Chief Downey needed some sea time. So, he sent him up the road to Boston to the cutter *Chase*, a three hundred and seventy eight foot high endurance cutter.

After two years on *Chase*, Chief Downey went to Station Woods hole as the Officer in Charge. From there he went back to a cutter, although a much smaller one, as the OIC of cutter *Towline* homeported in Bristol, Rhode Island.

In 1988, after only a Year on *Towline*, Chief Downey was asked to take command at Station Chatham to correct some "problems" there.

In 1989 he pinned on Senior Chief and five short years after arriving at Chatham, he headed across the sound for some "Island Time" at Station Brant Point. I asked Master Chief if there were any big rescues or sea stories from his time out at Station Brant Point and he thought for a minute and

Coast Guard cutter *Towline*. *USCG photo.*

said "Well, we did win the Nantucket Christmas Tree Decorating Contest five consecutive years…they even put it in my award."

And, sure enough, it was in there. Congrats Jack!

He also took Command of another unit, the cutter *POINT HANNON* for three months. Apparently, he was looking for a little challenge, and decided that two commands at once might do the trick.

But most notably, in the summer of 1994, Jack and Judith's first grandson, Jayson, was born. He'll be turning fourteen in a month, and it may be a bit early, but Happy Birthday Jayson! And before Master Chief would leave Brant Point, he'd see the birth of his second grandson, Justyn in January 1998.

That summer, after five years on Nantucket, Senior Chief Downey…wait a minute, five years, on NANTUCKET???? After just spending five years in CHATHAM???? What are we talking about "arduous service"…you spent ten years at two of the most visited vacation spots in the country!!! Sign me up.

Anyway, in the summer of 1998, Senior Chief Downey moved back to his hometown and took command of Station Point Judith. And in September of the same year, he put on his second star and was advanced to Master Chief Boatswain's Mate.

However, once again, he did not feel the service was challenging him to his full potential, so at various points over the next two years he took command of the cutter *Hammerhead* and Station Brant Point. That's right, count 'em, Three commands!!! It's like the board game "Risk," he just took over as much of the world as he could. A word of wisdom for you COs and OICs out there, if Master Chief Downey is in town, make sure you lock up your unit because the next morning you might find a new nameplate on your door and all your stuff out on the lawn.

After two short years, wow a two-year tour, must have been pretty rough on you, Jack…after two years at Station Point Judith, in 2000, Master Chief Downey headed all the way down to the Coast Guard Academy to teach at the Command and Operations School.

While there his first granddaughter, Tahlia was born, June 17th, 2001. She just turned the big number seven three days ago so we owe her a Big Happy Belated Birthday as well! Happy Birthday Tahla!

And in April 2004 the Downey's welcomed another grandson, D.J. to the family.

While at the LDC Master Chief, once again, found the opportunity to take command of the cutter *Hammerhead*. Apparently, he reaaaaally liked that boat.

So, after temporarily commanding her on three previous stints, we finally got the hint that cutter *Hammerhead* was where he really wanted to be and in 2004, he took Command of the cutter in Woods Hole. And he welcomed the newest members of the Downey Clan, Ava and Seamus in 2006.

And that is where he stayed until the summer of 2006 when I called him up and asked him to serve as the District One Command Master Chief. So, after forty-two years, twelve tours, five kids, and six grandkids later, here we are.

And in all of these assignments and years of service, Jack was never stationed farther south than New London, Connecticut. As mentioned, he did do law enforcement patrols on *Chase* to the Caribbean, but for the most part, he spent his entire career in the Northeast.…Oh, and then there was that time he coxswain'd a boat across the Delaware River for General George Washington…but other than that, it's been all New England.

Now here's the part where I came up a little short for Jack Downey. You see, I've already been talking for far too long, and usually, the speaker hits on some "operational highlights" during each of the tours. But, his service was far too distinguished, his accomplishments far too many, to do it justice.

So how do you pay proper tribute to a man whose career and life has been so embedded with that of this region? I could say things like "five thousand search and rescue cases" or "over 700 lives saved" but I do not think it gives the personal touch that Master Chief deserves. Instead, let's see what he did through some of the big events in New England over the last forty years and also mention some of the programs and policies that he shaped that now affect the entire Coast Guard.

During the Blizzards of 1978 Master Chief Downey stood the watch at Station Point Judith for members who were snowed in at their homes.

In 1980 he decided it made sense to work with fishermen to do dockside safety boardings instead of just waiting until they were offshore in the elements…sound familiar?

In July 1985, Chief Downey directed his boat crews and numerous civilian vessels in the recovery of one hundred and eight elderly passengers aboard the cruise ship *Pilgrim Belle* that sank off of Cuttyhunk Island.

While at Station Chatham, Master Chief developed, and hosted, the first Commercial Fishing Vessel Safety Symposium. These programs now dot the coast of New England annually and host thousands of fishermen and industry professionals each year.

While at Station Chatham during Halloween storm of 1991, later known as the "Perfect Storm," Master Chief and CWO Tom Guthlein "lasso'd" a fishing vessel that broke free of its mooring and safely secured it to the dock. Yup, "lasso'd." And they used the new hundred and fifty-six thousand dollar jet drive boat the station just got as a "fender" to cushion its collision with the dock…oops.

Without doctrine or guidance, his crews at Station Chatham were some of the first to wear Dry Suits because "it just seemed to make sense."

On *Hammerhead* in 1999, Master Chief responded to the crash of EgyptAir 990 which plummeted into the Atlantic Ocean sixty miles south of Nantucket.

That same year, his crews assisted rescue workers responding to the plane crash of John F. Kennedy Junior.

And shortly after September 11th, Master Chief was hand selected to take command of cutter *Hammerhead* to stand security watches in New York Harbor.

Ladies and Gentlemen, these are just a few of his many accomplishments. But what I'd like you to notice is that most of these talk of Jack Downey "leading" or "directing" his crews, or giving them an opportunity to achieve.

There's an 'ole Irish proverb that I think describes this well: "A society grows great—when leaders plant trees whose shade, they know, they shall never sit in."

In the Coast Guard we call this standing on the shoulders of those who have come before us in the Long Blue Line of expert seamen who have chosen a life serving our Country and protecting its shores and citizens.

However, in a career as distinguished and selfless as Jack's I do not think it fair to say that we are merely standing on his shoulders. In hundreds of cases, across the ranks and throughout the Coast Guard, Master Chief, whether directly or indirectly, has in some way or another *carried* each of us to where we, and the service, are today.

To give you just a glimpse of this impact we did a little staff work. Currently, in District One alone, there are:

Five Officers in Charge

Two Commanding officers, and

Four Executive Petty Officers…who worked directly for Master Chief Downey at some point in their career. Again, that's right now, in District One Alone.

But if you peel the onion back a little farther, you get what I like to call the Jack Downey effect. For example, Senior Chief Eric Baruzzi, Officer in Charge of Station Boston, worked for Chief Warrant Officer Tom Guthlein at Station Castle Hill. And Chief Warrant Officer Guthlein was Master Chief's XPO at Station Chatham.

So, indirectly, the Officer in Charge that Senior Chief Baruzzi is today, was influenced by Jack Downey.

But why stop there…

Lieutenant Mark Crysler, Executive Officer on cutter *Willow* worked for Chief Warrant Officer Doug Tribou (Triboo), aboard the cutter *Chokeberry*, and Chief Warrant Officer Tribou is currently the Commanding Officer of the cutter *Ida Lewis*. And *he* worked for Master Chief Downey at Station Point Judith.

Impressed huh? I'm just getting warmed up.…

Both Lieutenant Greg Somers and Lieutenant Junior Grade Patrick Ball, Commanding Officer and Executive Officer of cutter *Morro Bay*, worked for Chief Steve Worrell aboard the *Escanaba* and *Katherine Walker* respectively. Chief Worrell is now the XPO at Station New London, and He worked for LT Crysler at ANT Bristol, who worked for Doug Tribou, who worked for Master Chief.

Do you see where I'm going with this? Already that's sixteen COs, XOs, OICs, or XPOs who owe part of who they are professionally, to Jack Downey. And again, this is just in the FIRST DISTRICT...it speaks nothing of the hundreds of men and women he trained at the Leadership Development Center nor the thousands of other Coast Guard men and women that Master Chief mentored and instructed along the way.

And if you talk to any of these men and women, they all remember Jack Downey for not only WHAT he taught them, but HOW. And I think that the "how" is just as, if not more important than the "what." A reservist who worked for Master Chief said:

"*Jack Downey was very tough and he demanded the best from his people. During his many training sessions, he could challenge the most self-assured sailor. But, no matter how tough he was, you always had the sense that you were being trained by the best. And when you earned his approval, you truly felt there was nothing you couldn't do.*"

I truly believe that the legacy we leave behind in the Coast Guard is not what we do, but what we inspire others to achieve. We are fortunate to have a small enough service that great people can have a ripple effect throughout our organization that transcends Units, Sectors, Districts, or Areas. Jack Downey is a very large stone in our service and the true measure of his impact will not be felt for years to come. He is an anomaly that pushed the service, and those in it, a little higher than previously thought possible.

Which brings me back to that definition of "legend" I mentioned earlier: "*Legend: A story, or body of stories, handed down for generations and popularly believed to have a historical basis.*"

So is Jack Downey a legend in our service? That is not for us to say here today. However, it will be up to each and every one of us, through our commitment, our dedication, and our sacrifice to determine his legacy.

He has done his part. He has stood the watch for more than forty years.

Now it's our turn to take the helm, the Coxswain's chair, the OIC's office, or whatever other assignment you may have, and honor his service, and the sacrifice of his family, through our own.

So today we say fair winds and following seas to Master Chief Jack Downey.

An incredible mentor.

A committed friend.

And a damn good Coast Guardsmen.

Master Chief, on behalf of the men and women who have had the pleasure to call you "shipmate," on behalf of the thousands of Coast Guard men and women who owe part of their success to you, and on behalf of the countless families who will never know that the training YOU provided made the difference in saving their loved one's life, THANK YOU.

Your service to your shipmates, the Coast Guard, and to this nation can never be measured, but it will always be admired.

Best of luck to you, Judith, and the entire Downey clan as you embark on your next adventure.

Semper Paratus!

Master Chief, will you please join me at the podium for some formal recognition?

Appendix 9

DOWNEY'S ASSIGNMENTS

BMCM John E. "Jack" Downey
July 16, 1947–August 21, 2022

USCG, November 1966–June 2008
Douglas A. Munroe Award, 1990
First Joshua James Ancient Keeper, 2003

Unit Assignments

1966—Training Center Cape May
1967—CGC *Casco*
1967—Air Station Salem
1968—STA PT Judith (reserve and active duty)
a. 1979, assumed permanent command
1982—CGC *Chase* (chief of boat)
1984—STA Woods Hole (permanent)
1987—CGC *Towline* (65 tug) (permanent)
1988—STA Chatham (permanent)
1993—STA Brant Point (permanent)
1997—CGC *Point Hannon* (temporary command)
1998—STA PT Judith (permanent)
1998—Station Brandt Point (temporary command)

1999—CGC *Hammerhead* (temporary command)
1999—CG LORSTA Nantucket (temporary command)
2000—CG Academy
a. CGC *Hammerhead* (temporary command)
2004—CGC *Hammerhead* (87 WPB) (permanent)
2005—CGC *Tiger Shark* (temporary command)
2006—First District Command Master Chief
2008—Retired

NOTES

Epigraph

1. Oberstar, address to the House of Representatives.

Preamble

2. Galluzo, *By Resolution and Perseverance*.
3. Galluzo, *By Resolution and Perseverance*.
4. Galluzo, *By Resolution and Perseverance*, 17.
5. Noble, "Legacy."
6. U.S. Life-Saving Service Heritage Association, educational materials.
7. U.S. Life-Saving Service Heritage Association, educational materials.
8. Records of the Humane Society of the Commonwealth.
9. U.S. Life-Saving Service Heritage Association, educational materials.
10. U.S. Coast Guard, Joshua James Ancient Keeper Award Announcement.

Prologue

11. *Webster's Dictionary*.

Introduction

12. Gordon McClay, e-mail to the authors, March 22, 2024.

Chapter 1

13. John E. Downey, personal Steno Note Books, submitted to the authors, May 2024.
14. *U.S. Coast Guard News*, June 8, 2008.
15. Downey, personal Steno Note Books.
16. James and Michael Downey, phone interviews with the authors, March 12 and March 24, 2024.
17. Michael Downey phone interview.
18. James Downey phone interview.
19. Judith Downey, phone interviews with the authors, March 23, 2024, and April 15, 2024.
20. Captain Mark Campbell, e-mail to the authors, January 31, 2024.
21. John E. Downey, note to PCPO Jason Holm, personal archives, May 10, 2005.

Chapter 2

22. John E. Downey, USCG Letter of Commendation, July 16, 1976.
23. Captain Cicalese's recollection with Downey, circa 1988.
24. John E. Downey, USCG, Commendation Medal Citation, December 1981.

Chapter 3

25. Douglas G. Currier, USCG, letter of appreciation, July 21, 1982.
26. Brian Marks, e-mail to the authors, January 3, 2024.
27. Marks e-mail.
28. Marks e-mail.
29. Marks e-mail.
30. Kevin Quigley, e-mail to the authors, February 28, 2024.

31. Quigley e-mail.
32. Quigley e-mail.

Chapter 4

33. John E. Downey, USCG, Achievement Medal Citation, June 1987.
34. Downey, Achievement Medal Citation, June 1987.
35. Downey, Achievement Medal Citation, June 1987.
36. Downey, Achievement Medal Citation, June 1987.
37. Gordon McClay, interview notes, January–May 2024.
38. McClay interview notes.

Chapter 5

39. U.S. Coast Guard, Munro Award Criteria.
40. Sheila Lucey, e-mail to the authors, February 21, 2024.
41. Thomas Guthlein, interview with the authors, July 2, 2023.
42. Zimmerman, "QE2 on the Rocks."
43. John E. Downey, USCG Meritorious Service Medal Citation, May 1993.

Chapter 6

44. McClay e-mail.
45. Maurice E. Gibbs, Nantucket Life Saving Museum letter, December 1, 1994.
46. NTSB Marine Accident Report.
47. J.F. Murray, USCG, letter of appreciation, March 28, 1998.
48. Murray letter of appreciation.
49. W.R. Webster, coauthor, Group Commander, Woods Hole (at the time).
50. Webster, Group Commander.
51. John E. Downey, USCG, Commendation Medal Citation, July 2000.
52. M.C. Ponttieri, USCG, letter of appreciation, July 14, 2000.

Chapter 7

53. U.S. Coast Guard, Academy Command & Operations School, summary for the period June 1, 2002–May 31, 2003.
54. Superintendent, USCGA letter 5300, undated, Command & Operations School staffing.
55. Dan Precourt, e-mail to the authors, December 17, 2023.
56. Precourt e-mail.
57. Precourt e-mail.
58. Precourt e-mail.
59. Precourt e-mail.
60. Lucey e-mail.
61. Precourt e-mail.
62. Mitchell and Webster, Pendleton *Disaster*.
63. Mitchell and Webster, Pendleton *Disaster*.
64. Precourt e-mail.
65. Precourt e-mail.
66. USCGA, Chief Command and Operations School, first endorsement on BMCM Downey's letter 1326 of May 10, 2003, Assignment Year 2004, OINC Screening Panel.

Chapter 8

67. Captain Webster's recollections.
68. Niagara MISHAP Analysis Board Report, Annex O (Survivability), May 1, 2001.
69. Niagara MISHAP Analysis Board Report, Annex O (Survivability).
70. Niagara MISHAP Analysis Board Report, Annex O (Survivability).
71. Webster recollections.
72. Webster recollections.
73. Niagara MISHAP Analysis Board Report, Annex O (Survivability).
74. Commander, Group Woods Hole letter, May 2001.
75. RADM Alan M. Steinman, correspondence with the author, February 1, 2024.
76. U.S. Life-Saving Service Regulations.
77. U.S. Life-Saving Service Regulations.

Chapter 9

78. John E. Downey, USCG, Commendation Medal Citation, August 2006.
79. Downey Commendation Medal Citation.
80. John E. Downey, remarks to prospective chief petty officers, May 10, 2005.
81. Downey remarks.
82. K.J. Stillings, Lieutenant Colonel, USMC, letter of appreciation, August 26, 2005.
83. Steve Babcock, e-mail to the authors, January 5, 2024.
84. Christine Bouressa, e-mail to the authors, August 6, 2023.

Chapter 10

85. Timothy Sullivan, e-mail to the authors, January 22, 2024.
86. Skip Bowen, e-mail to the authors, January 5, 2024.
87. Bowen e-mail.
88. William R. James, e-mail to the authors, January 1, 2024.
89. James e-mail.
90. John E. Downey, USCG, Legion of Merit Citation, June 2008.

Chapter 12

91. Transcript of MCPO Downey's February 18, 2022 remarks at Chatham Bars Inn, December 16, 2024.
92. Transcript of Downey's remarks.
93. Bill Quinn Jr., interview with the authors, January 11, 2025.
94. Richard Ryder Jr., interview with the authors, January 11, 2025.
95. Heather Morin, e-mail to the authors, January 16, 2025.

Chapter 13

96. Kristen Bowen, oral history of MCPO Charles "Skip" Bowen, https://www.history.uscg.mil.
97. U.S. Coast Guard, "Top 10 All Time Rescues."

98. National Coast Guard History Museum Association, "Stories that Matter," 6.
99. Randolph, "For Men Only."
100. U.S. Coast Guard Historian, "Long Blue Line."
101. Commander, First Coast Guard District (OSR), letter 1650, October 26, 1970.
102. *New York Times*, "Rhode Island Boat Capsizes."
103. Emory, "Ferry with 442 Loses Steering."
104. NTSB letter to Scutter.
105. NTSB letter to Yost.
106. USCG Group Woods Hole, Letter of Commendation to BMCM John Downey, January 31, 2000.
107. John Downey, citation to accompany the USCG Commendation Medal Citation, Gold Star in lieu of a fourth, 2006.
108. U.S. Coast Guard, solicitation for the Cy23 Boat Forces Awards.
109. Bowen, oral history.
110. Bowen, oral history.

Appendix 2

111. U.S. Coast Guard, David H. Jarvis Award, https://www.dcms.uscg.mil.

Appendix 6

112. Bowen e-mail.
113. Thomas Botzenhard, letter to Downey, June 20, 2008.
114. Scott Backholm, letter to Downey, June 20, 2008.
115. Carlon Brietzke, letter to Downey, June 20, 2008.
116. D.J. Croyle, letter to Downey, June 20, 2008.
117. Bill Donahue, letter to Downey, June 20, 2008.
118. Karen Hanson, letter to Downey, June 20, 2008.
119. Kyle Takakjian, letter to Downey, June 20, 2008.
120. Colleen McCarthy, letter to Downey, June 20, 2008.

BIBLIOGRAPHY

Books

Galluzo, John. *By Resolution and Perseverance*. Humane Society of the Commonwealth of Massachusetts, 2022.

Mitchell, Theresa, and Russell Webster. *The* Pendleton *Disaster*. 3rd ed. The History Press, 2010.

Articles

Emory, Eugene. "Ferry with 442 Loses Steering Near Pier; Coast Guard Saves the Day." *Journal Bulletin*.

National Coast Guard History Museum Association. "Stories that Matter." Spring 2024.

New York Times. "Rhode Island Boat Capsizes and 12 Die." May 19, 1983.

Noble, Dr. Dennis. "A Legacy: The United States Life-Saving Service." uslife-savingservice.org.

Randolph, Ted. "'For Men Only': Tradition Broken 27 Years Ago by Mistake." *Alexander City Outlook*.

Zimmerman, Karl. "QE2 on the Rocks." *Martha's Vineyard Gazette*, July 25, 2022.

Government Agency Reports

Niagara MISHAP Analysis Board (MAB) Report. Annex O (Survivability), May 1, 2001.

NTSB letter to Admiral Paul Yost, July 24, 1986 (M-86-51 to M-86-66).

NTSB letter to Mr. Richard Scutter, Hyannis Harbor Tours, July 24, 1986.

NTSB Marine Accident Report, PB97-916401, NTSB/MAR-97/0l.

Oberstar, James L. Address to the House of Representatives. Vol. 154, no. 95 (June 10, 2008).

Records of the Humane Society of the Commonwealth.

U.S. Coast Guard. ALCOAST 034/24, R 251757Z JAN 24. Solicitation for the Cy23 Boat Forces Awards.

———. ALCOAST 060/21. Joshua James Ancient Keeper Award Announcement, February 19, 2021.

———. Munro Award Criteria, 2024.

U.S. Coast Guard, ALDIST. "Top 10 All Time Rescues." August 4, 2007.

U.S. Coast Guard Historian. "The Long Blue Line."

U.S. Life-Saving Service Heritage Association. Educational materials.

U.S. Life-Saving Service Regulations. Article VI, Section 252.

INDEX

D

E

F

G

H

I

J

K

L

M

N

O

P

Q

V

W

Authors Webster (*left*) and Cicalese at the First Annual Jack Downey Boat Forces Unit Awards, Portsmouth, New Hampshire, May 2024. *Authors' collection.*

ABOUT THE AUTHORS

Captain Webster retired from federal service in 2023 after serving forty-six years with the U.S. Coast Guard, the Transportation Security Administration and the Federal Emergency Management Agency. His final assignment was teaching future Coast Guard officers ethics, science and disasters and emergency management. He continues his work with two Department of Homeland Security Centers of Excellence, focusing on protecting soft targets like schools, houses of worship and sports stadia, and enhancing today's Coast Guard search and rescue preparedness and watchstander decision-making. He received the Department of Homeland Security Secretary's Award for outstanding performance in 2021 after he led the northeastern region during the COVID-19 pandemic. He is also the Coast Guard Academy's 2017 Distinguished Alumni and an International Association of Emergency Management Lifetime Certified Emergency Manager. *New England's Lifesaver* is his fifth nonfiction maritime history book. He resides in Plymouth, Massachusetts, with his wife, Theresa, and rescue dog, Willow.

Captain Cicalese retired from the U.S. Coast Guard in 2010 after serving for thirty years. He served at small boat stations; aboard cutters, patrol boats and buoy tenders; and in command staff positions, including during large emergency events such as the *Valdez* oil spill and Hurricane Katrina. He received the Seven Seal Award from the Employer Support of the Guard and Reserve for meritorious leadership and initiative in support of the men and women who serve America during his career on active and reserve duty. He continues to assist seafarers and veterans via several New England humanitarian organizations, including the Mariners House, Boston, where he served as executive director for nearly two decades, transitioning to the board; he also served as president, celebrating his twenty-fifth year of participation. He has also served as president of the Wardroom Club, Boston, transitioning to the board as the club's member-at-large. He lives in Duxbury, Massachusetts, with his wife, Julie, and their third rescue dog, Luca.